Articles in English as a Second Language

A Phraseological Perspective

Justyna Leśniewska

Articles in English as a Second Language
A Phraseological Perspective

Jagiellonian
University
Press

REVIEWER
Prof. David Singleton

COVER DESIGN
Marcin Klag

With the financial support of the Institute of English Studies of the Jagiellonian University

ISBN 978-83-233-4691-3

JAGIELLONIAN
UNIVERSITY
PRESS

www.wuj.pl

Jagiellonian University Press
Editorial Offices: ul. Michałowskiego 9/2, 31-126 Kraków
Phone: +48 12 663 23 80, Fax: +48 12 663 23 83
Distribution: Phone: +48 12 631 01 97, Fax: +48 12 631 01 98
Cell Phone: +48 506 006 674, e-mail: sprzedaz@wuj.pl
Bank: PEKAO SA, IBAN PL80 1240 4722 1111 0000 4856 3325

Contents

Introduction

> ... article usage in English is complex and, in many instances, arbitrary. There are several different uses for each article, articles are often omitted, and there are dialectal differences in the use of articles.
>
> (Brinton & Brinton, 2010, p. 123)

> ... the English article system... appears to be virtually impermeable to instruction.
>
> (Gass & Selinker, 2008, p. 383).

The aim of this book is twofold: firstly, to provide an overview of research findings on the acquisition and use of articles in English as a second language (L2); secondly, to investigate articles in L2 English from a phraseological perspective.

Learners of English as a second language are well known to experience numerous problems with mastering the article system. The extent of the problem depends heavily on the mother tongue of the learners and on other languages they may speak. Articles are particularly challenging for speakers of article-less languages such as Polish, Russian, Mandarin or Korean. Research on second language

acquisition (SLA), apart from confirming that problems with articles are strongly dependent on the first language (L1), also yields several other insights: that learners' problems are most pronounced at
the beginning stages of acquisition, that the indefinite article tends
to be acquired late, and that the definite article is often overused.
Also, there is evidence that, for some learners, articles remain a problematic area even at advanced – possibly even native-like – levels of
attainment.

No straightforward linguistic description can capture the functioning of the article system in English. A number of syntactic, semantic and pragmatic factors play a role in their use. Traditionally, articles are presented as elements of the morphosyntactic system of the
English language, which grammaticalizes the features of countability
and number. Equally important are semantic and pragmatic accounts
of the use of articles, since articles encode the notions of definiteness
and specificity, and play a major role in structuring information and
maintaining topic continuity in discourse. The central concept behind
the use of the definite article – definiteness – has a long history as
a topic of investigation not only in linguistics, but also in philosophy.
As a syntactic phenomenon, articles have been studied within the generative tradition as components of noun phrases (NPs) and even as
heads of determiner phrases (DPs). They have also been investigated
from a historical perspective, as well as in computational linguistics
studies, and in connection with natural language processing. There
is a vast collection of writings on articles that employ contrastive
and functional approaches, while the most recent work on articles
includes sociolinguistic approaches.

Given such a vast body of academic insights into the deceptively
modest-looking *a* and *the*, it remains a daunting, if not impossible,
task to try to offer a complete overview of the issues involved in the
study and description of the English articles. However, the first two
chapters of this book are intended to provide at least the essential,

basic information on existing linguistic accounts of the English articles, in order to provide a descriptive framework for the rest of the
book and to set the scene for further discussion. Chapter 1 thus provides an overview of the traditional descriptive treatments of the article, as they are found in grammars of the English language. The main
lines of linguistic inquiry into the English article system, which were
briefly mentioned above, are discussed in Chapter 2. This chapter presents an overview of the major aspects of article use that have been
investigated in long-standing approaches to the study of articles in
English, and the key notions in semantics and the philosophy of language which are relevant to the study of articles. To complement the
first two chapters, Chapter 3 summarizes the way various approaches
to language use have conceptualized the nature and role of the English
article, underscoring the fact that none of them manages to account
for all possible uses made by speakers of that language.

The complexity of the English article system highlighted in the
first three chapters makes it obviously a difficult aspect of the language for its learners. However, despite the uncontroversial character
of this observation, actually explaining the reasons for this state of
affairs is not a trite task. Since it is so commonplace to say that articles
are *difficult* for Polish learners of English, it seems worthwhile to take
a closer look at the concept of *difficulty* in second language research.
Chapter 4 applies this concept, as construed and operationalized in
the literature, to the English articles. The available theoretical frameworks allow for a detailed analysis of reasons why articles are such
a stumbling block for many learners. The topic of pedagogical rules
and their difficulty is connected to the important topic of explicit
knowledge and explicit learning, as contrasted with implicit knowledge and learning. Those concepts are also discussed in this chapter.

A more detailed overview of what is known about the acquisition
and use of articles in L2 English is provided in Chapter 5 of this book,
which discusses available research on this topic, bringing together

findings from various publications, despite the very different methodologies and various limitations of the discussed studies which reduce
their generalizability. As will be seen, the body of research on articles in SLA revolves mostly around the nature and extent of L1 influence, the role of Universal Grammar, semantic universals, the time
course of development, and ultimate attainment. Since L2 learning
often takes place in instructional contexts, Chapter 6 complements
Chapter 5 by discussing the way articles are treated in the teaching
of English to speakers of other languages.

While articles have been examined from a number of angles,
there is a perspective which has not received much attention in SLA
research, namely the role of phraseology in the acquisition and use
of articles. While the correct use of articles by learners of L2 English
is traditionally seen as the result of the eventual mastery of grammar
rules, it stands to reason that it may also be to some extent collocational in nature, i.e., it may be aided by the storage and retrieval of
prefabricated and/or conventionalized language chunks (of various
kinds). However, phraseological phenomena are very complex. While
interest in all kinds of formulaicity-related issues has been growing
rapidly in recent years, there is still no clarity as to how chunking and
formulaicity might interact with grammatical development. This is
why Chapter 7 presents the trends and main findings on the role of
phraseological phenomena in language use and examines their relevance to the case of the English articles.

Descriptive grammars of English, pedagogical materials, and
studies on learner language do include references to "idiomatic" or
"fixed" uses of articles. However, this category is invoked to account
only for those uses of the definite, indefinite or zero article which cannot be explained by the "rules." Consequently, formulaicity is simply a convenient label for those cases of article use which fall outside the rule-governed spectrum. My argument is that the interplay
between formulaicity in language and the use of articles is much more

complex than just the existence of some odd uses of articles frozen in idiomatic expressions. It is possible that the formulaic nature of language to some extent contributes to correct article use. This possibility is explored by means of two studies presented in Chapter 8. The findings of those studies indeed offer some support for the view that frequency-driven conventionality in language may play a role in the use of articles in L2 English.

CHAPTER 1

Articles: Descriptive approaches

1.1. INTRODUCTION

Traditional descriptive treatments of articles are by far the most widely used in language teaching. They inform a vast majority of textbooks, pedagogical grammars, and teaching materials. They are also important for studies on article acquisition and use in L2, though in research there is a greater variety of theoretical approaches, with a number of studies adopting the functionalist, generative, or cognitive approaches, as will be seen in Chapter 3 of this book.

In order to establish a descriptive framework for the discussion of articles, I will draw on a number of descriptive grammars of English. The two most often used sources will be referred to in an abbreviated form: the widely-used and influential comprehensive grammar entitled *The Longman Grammar of Spoken and Written English* (Biber, Johansson, Leech, Conrad, & Finegan, 1999) will henceforth be referred to as *Longman Grammar*, while the *Cambridge Grammar of the English Language* (Huddleston & Pullum, 2002) will be referred to as *Cambridge Grammar*. A result of a large cooperative project, the

Longman Grammar was very innovative in its day, as it was based on corpus-derived data. It remains a popular source of information and terminology for researchers in the field of SLA and for developers of language teaching materials. Regarding terminology, the *Longman Grammar* is mostly consistent with the classic *Comprehensive Grammar of the English Language* (Quirk, Greenbaum, Leech, & Svartvik, 1985). The *Cambridge Grammar* is another extensive and detailed description of the English language system, which in many ways departs from the *Longman Grammar* in terms of theory and terminological aspects.

1.2. THE CLASSIFICATION OF ARTICLES AS PARTS OF SPEECH AND SENTENCES

In descriptive grammars of English, articles are usually classified as belonging to the larger category of determiners, which are function words used to specify the reference of a noun (*Longman Grammar*, p. 259). Determiners, in turn, are studied as part of the noun phrase.

Various descriptive grammars use different terminologies to present the structure of the noun phrase (NP), or, as it is sometimes called, noun group (Downing & Locke, 1992). Barring differences in terminology, the structure of the NP in English is presented as consisting of pre-head elements, the head, and post-head elements. Determiners (and thus articles) figure among pre-heads and always precede other pre-head elements.[1]

---

[1]   This only applies to languages like English, i.e., those that are categorized as "head-first" languages in generative grammar. For languages that are "head-last," the sequencing is different.

The structure of the noun phrase is typically presented in the fashion illustrated below (Carter & McCarthy, 2006, p. 324):

pre-head		head	post-head	
determiners	premodifiers		complements	postmodifiers
a		*mother*	*of three children*	
his	*recent*	*claim*	*that he was innocent*	*which was broadcast on state radio and TV*

While complements (as their name suggests) complete the meaning of the noun phrase (as in *the mother of three little children, a rise in interest rates*), postmodifiers are either relative clauses or are modifiers that can be paraphrased as relative clauses (*the house nearby, the house which is nearby*).

The various classifications show divergences when it comes to post-head elements; for example, the noun phrase may be represented as (Greenbaum, 1991):

[determiners] [pre-modifiers] noun [post-modifiers]

or as (Kreidler, 1998):

[determiners] [modifier] head [complement].

Some sources use other terms, e.g. *modifier*, for all pre-head elements, and *qualifier* for post-head elements (Downing & Locke, 1992, p. 410), others classify all post-heads as postmodifiers except for appositive clauses (Greenbaum, 1991). Luckily, the first element of the noun phrase, the determiner, is the one for which there is no terminological confusion.

Even though specific typologies of determiners vary, generally speaking, determiners typically specify whether the reference is definite or indefinite (*the, a*), possessive (*my, her, etc.*), demonstrative (*this, those, etc.*), or they specify number or quantity (*three, first*) (Carter & McCarthy, 2006, p. 335).

For example, the *Longman Grammar* and Greenbaum (1991) divide determiners into the following categories, on the basis of their position inside the NP:

- pre-determiners (e.g. *all, both, half*; multipliers, e.g.: *double, once, twice*);
- central determiners: articles (*the, a[n]*), demonstrative determiners (e.g. *this, these*), possessive determiners (e.g. *his, her*);
- post-determiners: ordinal numerals, semi-determiners (*same, other, former, latter, last, next*), cardinal numerals, and quantifying determiners.

As Kreidler (1998) points out, the typical classification of determiners is essentially semantic in nature, as illustrated, for example, by the categories of demonstrative determiners (e.g. *this, these*), possessive determiners (e.g. *his, her*), quantifiers: specific (e.g. *five*), general (e.g. *much, several*), collective (e.g. *all*), distributive (e.g. *every*).

The *Cambridge Grammar*, in turn, makes a useful distinction between determiners and determinatives. A determiner is a function in the NP structure, whereas a determinative is a lexical category; a distinct, primary category. While it is true that the function of the determiner is usually realized by a determinative (e.g. *the, a, those*) or a determinative phrase (e.g. *too many, almost all*), it can be realized by a genitive noun phrase (as in *the minister's speech*). Determinatives, in turn, do not always function as determiners, they can also function in other roles, for example as modifiers. The following types of determiners are distinguished (*Cambridge Grammar*, p. 355):

1. basic determiners:
    - determinatives: **the** *tie,* **a** *book,* **those** *shoes*
    - determinative phrases: **almost every** *tie,* **at least two** *shoes*

2. subject-determiners:
   - genitive NPs: *my tie*, *the boy's shoes*

3. minor determiners:
   - plain NPs: *what colour tie*, *this size shoes*, *Sunday morning*, *tomorrow evening*
   - preposition phrases: *over thirty ties*, *up to thirty shoes*, *from ten to fifteen judges.*

As the name suggests, the determinatives are the basic type of determiners. The *Cambridge Grammar* distinguishes 14 main categories of determinatives (for example, personal, universal, distributive, disjunctive, *etc.*), of which articles are the first one (see the *Cambridge Grammar*, p. 356, for the complete list).[2]

1.3. THE INDEFINITE ARTICLE

The English indefinite article *a* (or *an* in the liaison form) is found only in a determiner function. The basic grammatical category relevant to the use of the indefinite article is number, since number corresponds to the semantic concept of countability, and the indefinite article can occur only with singular countable nouns. The two major grammatical types of nouns, count (or countable) and non-count (or non-countable) differ with respect to whether they can express contrast of number (Carter & McCarthy, 2006, p. 335). The most

---

2 As can be seen, traditional or descriptive approaches consider the article to be a component of the NP. However, as will be seen in Chapter 3, generative approaches in syntax posit the existence of DPs (determiner phrases) in which the determiner is the head, thus highlighting the importance of determiners.

common approach in descriptive grammars is to treat the count/ non-count distinction as based on the syntactic behaviour of nouns. As a consequence, the test for whether a noun is countable or not is its occurrence with cardinal numbers (*Cambridge Grammar*, p. 334). The distinction is, of course, to some extent motivated semantically, since the general principle is that count nouns denote entities which are treated as units, while non-count nouns denote entities which are treated as non-divisible, or that do not have clear boundaries (Carter & McCarthy, 2006, p. 335). However, this distinction cannot be made in a predictable manner on the basis of the physical properties of the entities denoted by nouns. This issue will be discussed in more depth in Chapter 2, section 4.

The indefinite article is the most basic indicator of indefiniteness, which can be understood as lack of identifiability: "with indefinite NPs, the addressee is not being expected to identify anything" (*Cambridge Grammar*, p. 371). The *Cambridge Grammar* (p. 372) distinguishes between two kinds of indefiniteness: quantitative and non-quantitative. Quantitative uses, for example in *I bought a new car, a cat just came into my house*, express existential quantification by indicating reference to one item. This use results from its historical origin as an unstressed variant of the numeral *one* (Hewson, 1964; Mitchell & Robinson, 1992). Non-quantitative uses, as in *Jill is a doctor*, where Jill is characterized as belonging to the class of doctors, indicate simple set membership. Generic uses of the determiner *a* are also always non-quantitative (*the lion is a ferocious beast*), and so are uses of *a* with count nouns (all examples in this passage are from the *Cambridge Grammar*). In many sources, the non-quantitative uses are labelled simply as "classification of an entity" and "generic use" (e.g. in the *Longman Grammar*, p. 260).

It is important to note that the English indefinite article encodes indefiniteness, not lack of specificity, so it can be used to introduce new entities (not previously mentioned, not identifiable to the listener) that are either specific or non-specific, as the following examples from Downing & Locke (1992, p. 429) illustrate:

- a new non-specific entity: *I need a new car*;
- a new specific entity: *I've bought a new car.*

References which follow the occurrence of a noun referring to a specific entity with an indefinite article usually take the form of definite noun phrases or personal pronouns:

> *A **cat** was the victim of a cruel attack when **she** was shot in the neck by **a pellet**. (…) The **pellet** went right through **the cat**'s neck and came out on the other side.*
>
> (*Longman Grammar*, p. 260)

Most of the complications in the use of the indefinite article arise from the complexities of the countability-related characteristics of nouns in English; for example, Downing and Locke (1992, pp. 422–423) enumerate six main different types of countability. This issue will be discussed further in Chapter 2, section 4. However, there are also some intricacies related to the notion of indefiniteness; for example, it is possible to use the indefinite article with proper nouns, which are definite by default, as in (examples from Downing & Locke, 1992, p. 430):

> *Is there a John Smith is this class?*
> *I can't imagine a Greece without an Athens.*
> *I've got a Goya at home, but it's only a reproduction.*

In such cases, the nouns refer to entities which are treated as members of a class, or "something abstract or imaginary is predicated" about them, or they are used as metonyms.

1.4. THE DEFINITE ARTICLE

As its name suggests, the definite article's main role is to indicate definite entities, i.e., ones that are known, familiar, or identifiable to the speaker and the hearer. This is a very general statement; the notion of definiteness is complicated and a topic of much discussion in various schools of linguistics, as will be explained in the next chapter. This section will present only the most basic facts about the definite article.

The definite article is compatible with all types of common nouns: count singular, count plural, and non-count, as illustrated by the following utterances:

> *I'm getting the screwdriver.*
> *I'm getting the shelves.*
> *I'm getting the paint.*

Specific types of uses of *the* are variously classified by different sources; however, by putting together a number of accounts offered by different descriptive grammars, we arrive at a set of roles that are most often played by the definite article. Before they are listed, it should be noted that a useful distinction is made by Downing and Locke (1992, p. 431) between definiteness which is identified endophorically (i.e., within the text) and exophorically (i.e., outside the text). Three of the common functions of the definite article, listed below, are exophoric, i.e., their definiteness results from what is known about the outside world, and the speakers' knowledge:

1. The referent being unique in the wider discourse (*the sun, the sky*).

2. The uniqueness of a specific entity in a given situation, for a specific speaker and a specific hearer, who share the non-linguistic

context. In the sentence *The President has been assassinated*, the determined noun phrase "the President" is most likely identifiable because of the specific context in which this message is being communicated. With an utterance like *Be quiet, or you'll wake up the baby!*, the interlocutors know which baby may be woken up.

3. The deictic role of the article (dependent on the situational context). In sentences like *Put the vase on the table, Could you do something about the noise?*, the referent is assumed to be identifiable on the basis of the physical or social context.

Other commonly recognized roles of the definite article, listed below, appear to be endophoric:

1. Indicating the identifiability of referents denoted by nouns which are modified, either by means of pre-modification (*the red dress*), or by means of post-modification or complementation (*the blue t-shirt at the bottom of the pile, the man who was the last one to exit the station*). The latter type of identification is sometimes called "cataphoric" (i.e., forward-looking), since the modifying element comes after the noun (e.g. *Cambridge Grammar*).

2. The anaphoric (i.e., "backward-pointing") role of the definite article: the entity is identifiable because it has been mentioned previously in the same discourse (e.g. Brinton & Brinton, 2010, p. 123). In other words, it could be called the rule of prior mention: the referent of the noun phrase is assumed to be known to the speaker because of the preceding reference. This kind of reference is sometimes labelled as direct anaphoric reference, as it involves the repetition of the same noun head, but with the definite article. (*We were approached by a young girl and an old woman; The girl looked distressed.*) However, as will be seen later in this book, this

description of article use is not entirely sufficient, as immediate anaphoric reference is in many cases more likely to be expressed by a pronoun (for a discussion of the as an indicator of a low level of accessibility, see section 3.3).

3. Indirect anaphoric references. Other types of anaphoric references are variously classified. I will use the label "indirect anaphoric references" (e.g. Kreidler, 1998, p. 148) as it seems to make the most sense when applied to uses like the one below, which involves synonymy:

I saw a strange picture on the wall. The painting was of the most unusual kind.

Likewise, the indirect anaphoric link between co-referential nominals may be based on other semantic relationships, for example meronymy or hyperonymy (Halliday & Hasan, 1976, p. 278). There is also the special case of references which some sources label "bridging references" (Clark 1977, cited in Saeed, 2003, p. 203). They can be illustrated with the following examples:

The car wouldn't start. The battery was flat.
I had two hours to kill before the conference began, so I went out for a walk. The park was beautiful.

The above examples illustrate how the listener is expected to create links with the preceding sentences by referring to general knowledge. The assumption is that the hearer can make the necessary implicature to relate a new reference to a previous one and establish coherence. In the first example, both the car and the battery are mentioned in the text, but exophoric knowledge about the battery as part of a car is required to understand the connection between the two.

This phenomenon of bridging will be discussed in more detail in section 3.3, which is devoted to cognitive treatments of articles.

The concept behind the above uses of the definite article is labelled as *identifiability* by the authors of the *Cambridge Grammar*. Identifiability occurs when only one relevant entity is assumed to satisfy the description expressed in the noun phrase. This identifiability of the referent may be established through a number of different means; for example, identifiability by virtue of uniqueness characterizes the following utterances:

Where did you put the keys?
Where did you put the milk?

They are identifiable because the speaker has in mind a certain specific set of keys, a specific carton of milk.

Contrary to the indefinite article, which occurs only as a determiner, the definite article has yet another syntactic function (beside that of a determiner): a modifier in constructions with superlatives and comparatives (*Cambridge Grammar*, p. 371).

The *Longman Grammar* also introduces the category of "idiomatic" uses of the definite article, but it is the briefest of mentions. Finally, the *Cambridge Grammar* also mentions that *the* to some extent also expresses totality, which means that it indicates the entire set or quantity of the items or substance which are referred to (even though the concept of totality is somewhat weaker than that expressed by universal quantification).

1.5. THE ZERO ARTICLE / BARE NOUN PHRASE

Most traditional descriptive grammars of English use the term *zero article* to refer to the absence of an article before a noun. For example, the *Longman Grammar* defines the zero article as one that occurs with uncountable nouns in contexts corresponding to the use of the indefinite article with countable nouns, as well as with plural countable nouns. However, the *Cambridge Grammar* and some other grammars, for example, *The Collins Cobuild English Grammar* (Sinclair, 1990) do not include the zero article in their descriptions of the article system.[3] Rather, they speak of conditions where the nominal (a unit intermediate between a noun phrase and a noun) can head the noun phrase without a determiner. In the *Cambridge Grammar*, the noun phrases containing a determiner are called *determined noun phrases*, while *bare noun phrases* are formed, under certain circumstances, by nominals in the absence of a determiner. Nominals headed by plural count nouns, or by non-count nouns can freely be admitted as indefinite by default. The examples from the *Cambridge Grammar* are as follows:

> *New cars were stolen.* – bare noun phrase (indefinite by default)
> *Two new cars were stolen.* – determined indefinite noun phrase
> *The new cars / Ally's new cars were stolen.* – determined definite noun phrase.

At first it may seem that the use or non-use of the term "zero article" is just a matter of terminology. However, as Berezowski (2009) explains, the concept of zero article is rooted in historical and structural linguistics. The term came into being as an explanation for why

---

[3]   In fact, the concept of the zero article is in itself problematic and not universally recognized by linguists (see Berezowski, 2009).

there is no article with some nouns, even though the use of articles in English is generally obligatory. The missing article was conceived of as existing but realized without an overt form. Berezowski argues that the situation is different: the English article system has not fully evolved, and articles are not used in all grammatical environments (2009). I will use the term *zero article* for the sake of convenience, simply to denote a missing article, as this kind of use seems to be the most common in the literature, also in language teaching.

In the case of singular count nouns, the inclusion of a determiner is generally obligatory. However, there are special cases of nouns which otherwise behave like ordinary countable nouns, but which in some phrases appear within a bare noun phrase; that is, they take the zero article. This happens, for example, to names of meals when they are used in a general sense, and names of places/institutions such as school, hospital, jail, *etc.* In the sets of sentences below, this use is contrasted with the ordinary, countable use of the same nouns.

We are going out for dinner.	*The dinner was delicious.*
He is in hospital, awaiting surgery.	*The hospital is located on the outskirts of the city.* *The surgery lasted two hours.*
The ceremony took place in church.	*The church is known for its beautiful altar.*
I worked in the evenings while I was at university.	*The university is building a new campus.*
She knew she would go to jail if they caught her.	*The car was parked outside the jail.*

The zero article is also used with means of transport and with relation to communication used in a general sense. This use, restricted to prepositional phrases opening with *by*, affects nouns that are both countable and uncountable: *go by bus/car/coach/plane/sea/taxi/train, travel by air/car/horse/train, contact by radio/telephone, send by mail/ post.* (But: *she took the train to Warsaw, it was in the mail, the telephone was black*). Other typical uses of the zero article include times of day (*at dawn, at night* (but: *she waited for the dawn, it was in the middle of the night*), days of the week (unless there is postmodification), months, seasons, and vocatives.

Another context in which the zero article is used is with some predicatives that have a unique reference. While English normally requires an article with singular countable nouns in a predicative position, the use of predicative noun phrases which name a unique role or position is quite common with the zero article, especially with the nouns *president* and *chairman*. Biber et al. found that uses such as *he was re-elected OPEC president in November*, with the nouns *chairman* and *president*, outnumbered *the chairman / the director* by about 5 to 1 (1999, p. 262).

Another use of the zero article which is extremely interesting is its occurrence in parallel structures (*between lawyer and client, father to son, door to door*). The *Longman Grammar* makes the following comment about this phenomenon: "as these nouns are countable, we would normally expect an article. Examples of this kind are often frozen idiomatic expressions, as in *from start to finish, from time to time, eye to eye, face to face*" (p. 263). Consequently, we are dealing here with a set of exceptions to a rule. Those exceptions are cases where the use occurs in fixed idiomatic elements of language. In other words, the production of an expression in its entirety, as a fixed phrase, overrides the need to insert an article where it should normally appear. We could treat all the manifestations of this phenomenon as nothing more than cases of idiomatic expressions containing usage which is not usual outside those idiomatic expressions. But there is more to this phenomenon: there is a pattern here which may be productive, in that when completely new structures are generated, one may say, for example, *I made the repairs, armchair by armchair*.

There is also a special use of the zero article which is completely genre-dependent, namely, its use in newspaper headlines, notices, and user guides, which is what the *Longman Grammar* calls "block language": *Cat finds treasure, insert batteries here.*

1.6. CONCLUSIONS

Some conclusions can be drawn from the above review. Firstly, the descriptions of the article system in English are extremely extensive and complicated. Secondly, there are very substantial differences between the available descriptive grammars in terms of taxonomy and terminology. Thirdly, all the rules abound in exceptions.

From a language learning perspective, the fact that there are so many different possible explanations of why *a* or *the* is used in a specific context is already very challenging. To make matters worse, none of the different explanations may make sense in a specific context. For example, let us consider the last definite article of the following sentence: *The insurgent was spotted looking out the window.* The referent "window" lacks definiteness, and the use of a definite article cannot be accounted exophorically or endophorically: the referent is not unique, even in that specific context (the building where the insurgent was may have had several windows), *the* serves no deictic purpose, the window is not readily identifiable, there is no direct or indirect anaphoric reference involved, no bridging reference is made possible, and reference cannot be made by means of meronymy or hyperonymy.

Another issue is the fact that the numerous exceptions to the rules are usually assumed to be idiomatic, in the sense of being fixed over time through continuous use. However, such "conventional" uses may nevertheless be productive to some extent, as for example, the use of the zero article in parallel structures, which enables one to say, for example, *the technicians removed the virus laptop by laptop.*

Above all, several facts suggest that the way article usage has traditionally been described in grammar books may be inefficient or insufficient to account for the full range of article uses. The following chapters will move beyond descriptive approaches to see if other traditions have succeeded in capturing the elusive nature of the rules that govern the use of articles.

CHAPTER 2

Key concepts
in the study of articles

2.1. INTRODUCTION

The previous chapter has shown that even basic descriptive accounts of article use are very complex, with seemingly more exceptions than regularities. This chapter attempts to answer the question of why this is the case, by looking first at some crucial concepts which underlie article use, namely reference, information flow, countability and definiteness.

2.2. REFERENCE

The use of articles is inextricably related to the notion of reference. A basic concept in semantics is the difference between a referring expression and its referent. The latter is a certain entity outside of the realm of language, and the former is the expression used to refer

to that entity (J. Lyons, 1977, p. 177).[4] The difference between the
two is the source of humour in the following joke and the cause of
the oddity of the following sentence (examples from Kreidler, 1998,
p. 131): *Question: Where can you always find sympathy? Answer: In
a dictionary, Washington has three syllables and 600,000 inhabitants*,
or in the saying *The dictionary is the only place where success comes
before work.*

Referents can be classified on the basis of a number of characteristics. One basic distinction is between fixed (also called constant)
referents and variable referents.[5] Fixed reference occurs when the referent is a universally unique entity (independently of context), as in
Lake Erie. Variable reference characterizes those referring expressions
whose referents may be different every time they are used, as in *we
swam in a lake.* The referent of a noun phrase which has variable reference is established on the basis of a variety of sources of information,
including context (both physical and linguistic), general knowledge,
etc. However, it is possible for nouns with fixed reference to be used
with variable reference, as in these examples: *every city has a Green-
wich village, this fellow is an Einstein, no Shakespeare wrote this play*
(Kreidler, 1998, p. 135).

In fact, the fixedness of reference appears not to be absolute: even
with expressions that are normally classified as having a fixed reference, for example, *the Eiffel Tower*, it is possible for that expression in
a sentence, for example, *look at the Eiffel Tower* to refer to a model of

---

4   Saeed (2003, p. 26) introduces a different definition of "referring expression."
     To him, a referring expression is a nominal (name or noun phrase) which has
     a non-generic interpretation. Generic uses are thus, confusingly, labelled as
     non-referring.
5   Considerable confusion results from the fact that the terms "unique" / "non-
     unique" are sometimes used to refer to this distinction. I find this extremely
     problematic, because uniqueness is also used interchangeably with specificity
     by some writers.

the famous tower, or a piece of jewellery that is shaped to resemble it, or to the half-size copy that stands in Las Vegas.

Another important distinction exists between specific and non-specific reference. In a sentence such as *I have a cat*, reference is made to a specific cat. On the other hand, in a sentence like *I'd love to have a cat*, the cat in question is most likely non-specific. Under some circumstances, a referring expression can even have two referents, one that is specific and one that is non-specific. An example of that possibility was imagined by Donnellan (1968), who hypothesized someone saying: *Smith's murderer is insane*. One interpretation is that of a non-specific referent: the speaker does not know who killed Smith, but in his opinion the person was insane. Another possible interpretation involves a specific referent: the murderer can be a specific person whose identity is known and who is known to be insane.

Finally, it is possible to contrast generic reference with non-generic reference, as illustrated by the following pairs of sentences (some examples taken from Kreidler 1998, p. 141):

> *A dog is a fine pet. / A dog is lying in the middle of the street.*
> *Dogs are fine pets. / I can hear dogs barking in the distance.*
> *The dog was man's first domestic animal. / The dog really frightened me.*

Generic reference is usually expressed by means of the zero article, but it can be expressed also through the use of a singular countable noun with either the definite or the indefinite article, as shown in the examples above. It is interesting to note that corpus analyses reveal generic uses to be relatively uncommon (less than 5% of all article uses, according to the *Longman Grammar*).

2.3. INFORMATION FLOW

The way in which articles are used in general terms depends on the information flow in discourse. Low (2005, cited in Głaz, 2012) makes a useful distinction between anaphoric-oriented and accessibility-oriented approaches to definiteness. Anaphoric-oriented approaches are centred on discourse: the motivation of the definite article is to be found in the preceding discourse. These approaches are very important in the structuring of the information flow in discourse. Accessibility-oriented approaches, for their part, are based on the notions of familiarity (or identifiability), with the crucial feature being the extent to which the referent is assumed to be known to the hearer.

In any clause, there are elements which present new information ("the new"), and elements which present information available from the preceding discourse ("the given"). The distribution of articles in corpora reflects what the *Longman Grammar* calls the "information principle": there is a preferred distribution of information in a clause, "corresponding to a gradual rise in information load" (p. 896). A consequence of that principle is that it is more usual for clauses to open with given information and continue to reveal new information. Adherence to the information principle contributes to the cohesion of a text. Reliance on this principle speeds up language production for the speaker and facilitates the processing of speech for the listener.

The information principle is also reflected in the distribution of articles in texts. According to the *Longman Grammar* (p. 269), across registers, definite articles are much more common in noun phrases which are in the subject position or which are the complement or object of a preposition than in phrases which are in the object position. For indefinite articles, the situation is reversed, which is in keeping with the fact that the object comes in the clause that is typically associated with new information. This kind of evidence provided by analyses of text corpora confirms that the distinction between the given and the new is indeed a guiding principle behind the structuring of discourse. However, there are always numerous exceptions to this rule, as will be seen in the section devoted to the treatment of articles in cognitive linguistics.

Of importance to the issues discussed in this book is the fact that while definiteness as a semantic and pragmatic category is closely related to the definite article in languages with article systems, it has been observed that article-less languages have other means of expressing definiteness, ranging from information flow and structure to word order and the use of some nominal and verbal categories, such as aspect (for an in-depth treatment of this topic, see C. Lyons, 1999). Firbas (1992) develops the theory of functional sentence perspective (FSP), which originated in the Prague school of linguistics, in order to explain how the semantics, grammar, the context of a sentence, as well as prosodic aspects, all contribute to a certain "orientation" or "perspective" of the sentence, in which some elements are more prominent than others. For Polish, this issue was investigated by Szwedek (1973), who showed how Polish displays a tendency to mark the definiteness of nouns by means of their sentence-initial placement. The positioning of the noun in mid-sentence or at the end is often interpreted as conveying indefiniteness.

2.4. COUNTABILITY

2.4.1. THE COUNT / NON-COUNT DISTINCTION

Countability is a concept of high importance for the use of the indefinite article. As was said above, the use of articles depends on the distinction between countable (also called "count") and uncountable (also called "non-count" or "mass") nouns. It is possible to describe all nouns in the English language in terms of their countability. This distinction appears quite unproblematic at first; Palmer called it "a fairly clear one" (1981, p. 127).

However, the count/non-count distinction, which is reflected in the syntax and semantics of nouns, verbs, adjectives, and quantifiers, is characterized by notable crosslinguistic variation and has been the subject of much discussion in linguistics and in the philosophy of language. It is interesting to look at how this seemingly unproblematic distinction is at the heart of a major debate about some of the core beliefs concerning the nature of the relationship between language and reality.

Some linguists do not differentiate between count and non-count nouns because "nouns display a range of 'countability'" (Kreidler, 1998, p. 137). Kreidler, for example, speaks of the "non-countable end of the continuum" (1998, p. 138). This view is problematic in that in any particular instance of use, a noun is either treated as countable or not, so from a grammatical point of view the distinction is a dichotomy. A grammar-based distinction between the two classes is presented in Palmer (1981, p. 126):

> Formally the two classes are easily distinguished. Count nouns alone may occur in the singular with the indefinite article *a*, while only mass nouns may occur with no article or with the indefinite quantifier *some*.

Palmer thus treats the indefinite article as actually defining what is countable or what is not countable, because the distinction between count/mass in English can be made on the basis of what article a word can be used with: those lexemes which take the indefinite article are countable. This reasoning is somewhat circular, as the use of articles is usually considered to be dependent on the count/mass status of nouns.

He argues strongly that the membership of nouns in the count or non-count categories is arbitrary:

> The semantic difference between these two classes is clear enough. The count nouns "individuate" – they indicate individual specimens, while the mass nouns refer to a quantity that is not individuated in this way. But the distinction does not correspond closely to any semantic distinction in the world of experience, and this should be no cause for surprise. (…) But there is no explanation in semantic terms why we can refer to a single mass of jelly as a jelly but not to a mass of butter as a butter.
>
> (Palmer, 1981, p. 126)

To Palmer, whether a noun belongs to both the count and the mass category is arbitrary and unpredictable. He gives the example of *cake*, which can be count as well as non-count, contrasted with *bread*, which is only non-count, even though you can get separate loaves of it. "A foreigner," writes Palmer, in one of very rare mentions of the foreign-language perspective, "could not guess, then, whether such words as *soap, trifle, cheese*, would be count nouns in English. He has, moreover, to learn the "individuating" nouns: *loaf of bread, cake of soap, pat of butter*" (Palmer, 1981, p. 127).

Thus, in Palmer's view, countability and uncountability are grammatical categories. While they tend to correspond to real-word properties of entities, they do not always do, as can be shown by both the differences in the distribution of the count/mass distinction across languages, but also by the inconsistencies within the same language (*wheat* vs. *oats*, for example).

While it seems that some nouns may belong to both categories, Palmer treats such nouns as belonging either to the "mass" category, while the uses of these nouns with an indefinite article are simply a kind of individuation that can be applied to them for specific purposes, for example, to denote a specific kind, or, with liquids, a familiar amount (as in *a coffee* meaning *a cup of coffee*), or to the "count" category, for example in the case of animals, can sometimes be used in the non-count manner, indicating meat (therefore the meaning of *could I have some cat* is clear, even though it is not customary to eat cat meat).

In the *Semantics of Grammar*, Wierzbicka (1988) includes an interesting discussion of countability, offering an argument against the axiom that the relationship between the count status of nouns and its meaning is arbitrary. She argues that form-classes are semantically motivated, and that "differences in grammatical behaviour reflect iconically differences in meaning" (1988, p. 501). Often referring to various languages, she argues that there always is an underlying justification behind the count status of nouns in a language. Brussels sprouts are countable because their size is just right, watermelon is too big, rice – the particles are too small. Onions are (or at some point were) more likely to be eaten as a whole, thus they are countable, garlic – less likely, hence uncountable. Prototypical fruits, such as apples, are likely to be countable in most languages. She tries to explain the differences between languages with references to eating habits: "people (in Russia) normally eat cucumbers raw, holding them individually in one hand, as one eats an apple or a banana, they don't chop and cook them…" (Wierzbicka, 1988, p. 504). It is true that different languages reflect different ways of conceptualizing the world: "The different conceptualizations have their own logic, which grammar reflects and illuminates" (Wierzbicka, 1988, p. 509). Indeed, a contrastive analysis of the semantics of foodstuffs in different languages tells us that there are a number of different possibilities for conceptualization.

The example Wierzbicka gives when discussing solids with a double (both count and non-count) status, *chocolate* vs. *soap*, is actually an excellent counter-argument to what she proposes. Soap cannot be conceptualized in terms of individual objects. A cake of soap is regarded as a piece of uncountable soap. Chocolates, on the contrary, can be visualized as individual entities. This has to do, according to Wierzbicka, with their fundamental qualities: a chocolate has an attractive appearance as a whole, and dimensions suitable to be eaten as one bite. Soap, on the other hand, can be viewed as "infinitely divisible": a piece of soap divided into parts will not lose its function as soap (1988, p. 510). It seems that Wierzbicka's argument has explanatory power in a diachronic sense: we can easily imagine that the first bars of soap were considered in English to be just lumps or chunks of some bigger mass, and this perception stuck and is reflected in the language. Nevertheless, this does not change the fact that from a contemporary perspective, there is hardly any difference between a pretty chocolate bar and nicely packaged piece of soap. In fact, bars of soap are similar in size and shape more than chocolates, so *a soap* may produce a clearer mental image than *a chocolate*.

Her argument is that what seems arbitrary is actually not; it is true that grammar does not reflect objective properties of entities in the real world, because it reflects human conceptualization. That is a very good point. But even when we accept, as Wierzbicka says, that "grammar reflects the human perception of the world and human anthropocentric interests" (1988, p. 520), there is still no predictive power to such an explanation. Even if a learner of English takes a very careful look at a bar of soap and a chocolate, there is no way to figure out which is countable and which one is not. We can come up with an explanation of why *watermelon* in uncountable (too big to be eaten as a whole), but that does not mean that all things too big to be eaten as a whole will be uncountable. Such post-hoc explanations do not translate into any kind of predictive power which would be of use in linguistic descriptions of how articles are used in a language.

Another example for the search for some kind of reality-based justification of the idiosyncratic countability behaviour of some nouns can be found in the *Cambridge Grammar*, which gives the following explanation of why some nouns, such as *dregs, grits, oats* only have the plural form. They denote substances consisting of particles, and they have no singular form because the individual particles are of no significance. They are different from non-count singulars (like *sand, gravel, rice, sugar*) because "the particles tend to be relatively larger in the case of the plural nouns (i.e. relative to the total amount of substance under consideration)" (p. 342). This is somewhat far-fetched – rice has bigger particles than dregs, and there are no reasons to believe it is necessarily considered in larger quantities.

The *Cambridge Grammar* distinguishes between count and non-count nouns, with the former denoting entities that can be counted (as tested by occurrence with cardinal numbers). In the *Cambridge Grammar*, chocolate as a count and non-count noun is treated as a case of polysemy (chocolate has more than one sense). It is common for nouns to have a count and non-count interpretation; the authors of the *Cambridge Grammar* call it "a widespread phenomenon." The fact that some nouns (for example, *piece*) have no established non-count uses, and some, like crockery, have no established count uses, does not matter: "these are simply the limiting cases" (p. 335). Count nouns denote what they call "atomic" entities, and non-count nouns are either substances which are not inherently bounded (*water*), or they are a heterogeneous aggregate of parts (*crockery, bedlinen, furniture, luggage*). This approach does not seem to account for the existence of non-count nouns such as *upholstery*.

2.4.2. IMPLICATIONS FOR L2 ACQUISITION

The differences in the conceptualization and lexicalization of countability across languages suggest considerable difficulties in second language learning. The count/non-count distinction seems to be present in most languages, and there are some common trends (for example, a substance is likely to be non-count), but there are many differences. In English, *furniture* is a non-count singular, *contents* is a non-count plural; in French it is the other way round (*meubles, contenu*). In English, *advice* and *information* are conceptualized as substances, in Polish and French they are countable. It is not surprising that a learner of English as a foreign language transfers the conceptualization of the referent from one language to another, and accordingly says "an information."

A study by Yoon (1993) showed that native speakers of English, when asked to classify nouns (which were presented out of context) with respect to their countability, were not unanimous in their judgements. This might not seem very surprising, as most nouns can function as either countable or not. In the same study, in a subsequent task, the same native speakers were nevertheless entirely successful in choosing the correct article to use with the nouns. Despite the methodological limitations of this study, it points to a certain problem: the level of metalinguistic knowledge, as well as the level of agreement, related to article use among native users of the language may be lower than for other aspects of the language system.

2.4.3. SOME USES OF ARTICLES ARE VERY DIFFICULT TO EXPLAIN

In many cases the use of the indefinite article seems to be in contradiction to the basic rules concerning countability. However, various instances of such "violations" differ in the extent to which they form certain patterns or regularities. For example, the use of primarily non-count nouns in a count sense can sometimes be quite regular, as in the case of drinks, which easily and regularly allow a count interpretation as in a serving (a bottle, a cup) of the drink (*I don't like beer / She offered me another beer*).

Similarly, nonce substance interpretations of primarily count nouns are also quite understandable, as in this example:

The termite was living on a diet of book.

(*Cambridge Grammar*, p. 337)

However, some interesting unpredictable cases are discussed under the heading of "abstract and event instantiations" in the *Cambridge Grammar* (p. 337): while many abstract nouns which have a primary non-count meaning can be used in secondary count senses denoting an event which constitutes an instance of the abstract concept, some do not, and this is *not* predictable, as shown by the following pairs of sentences (examples from the *Cambridge Grammar*):

Considerable injustice was revealed during the enquiry.
*Two fundamental injustices were revealed during the enquiry.
Serious harm was done to the project's prospects.
*Two serious harms were done to the project's prospects.

The same goes for abstract nouns derived from verbs, as illustrated by the following examples:

discussion – discussions
permission – *permissions
Full discussion of the land question is vital.
Two discussions of the land question took place.
Permission was required.
*Two separate permissions are required.

Finally, it should be mentioned that while countability is the main criterion which enables the correct use of the indefinite article, there are some cases when the indefinite article is used in structures with countable plural nouns, as in:

A very pleasant three days was spent with Kim's aunt in Brighton.
                                                        (Cambridge Grammar)

The explanation offered by the *Cambridge Grammar* is that the NP containing the plural form is construed as singular, by virtue of denoting a continuous stretch of time.

While with definite count singular NPs, identifiability is normally ensured by the fact that there is only one entity that satisfies the description in the head of the phrase, as noted in the *Cambridge Grammar* (p. 370), under certain circumstances, the definite article can be appropriate with a count singular even when the context does not strictly limit the number of entities satisfying the description given in the nominal to just one:

Put down the cup on the arm of your chair.
He married the daughter of his bank manager.

This is very counter-intuitive, as the latter sentence does not mean that the bank manager had only one daughter.

Another example of one more strange use of articles which linguists try to explain is illustrated by the following examples:

He took the child by the hand.
He grabbed me by the arm.
She hit him in the face.

This usage is possible only with the referent being prototypically a body part (cf. *(?) *She grabbed me by the tie, Cambridge Grammar*, p. 370). Secondly, "the body-part NP and the NP with which it is associated are respectively oblique and direct complements of a single verb," which explains why this kind of interpretation is not possible in the case of *I used the arm to help me get over the fence* (*Cambridge Grammar*, p. 370).

Let us consider this example from the *Cambridge Grammar* (p. 339):

Jill has a good knowledge of Greek.

This sentence is correct, even though knowledge is a clearly non-count noun: it has no established plural and combines with determinatives such as much, little, enough (as in *they have little knowledge of the matter*). The explanation we find in the Cambridge Grammar is that the function of the indefinite article is to "individuate a sub amount of knowledge, her knowledge of Greek." However, as the authors note, "this individuation does not yield an entity conceptualized as belonging to a class of entities of the same kind" (p. 339), so the following sentences are not acceptable (p. 339):

*Jill has an excellent knowledge of Greek and Liz has another.
*They both have excellent knowledges of Greek.

From a language-learning point of view, the crucial aspect concerning article use and countability is whether a certain observable pattern is generalizable, that is, whether it constitutes a productive "rule." Certain patterns in the use of articles, even if very subtle, are at least regular. Others seem to be completely arbitrary.

2.5. DEFINITENESS

Definiteness is a concept that has been much discussed in semantics and in the philosophy of language, which deals with the logic of the notion of definiteness, and the truth values of definite descriptions. In the early 20th century, Russell (1905) classified definite noun phrases as "definite descriptions," and this term continues to be used, even without commitment to Russel's views on definiteness (Neale, 1990). Neale (1990) offers an in-depth analysis of Russell's framework.

An early study on articles from a diachronic perspective was published by Christophersen (1939), who introduced the notion of familiarity in the study of definiteness: "the article the brings it about that to the potential meaning (the idea) of the word is attached certain association with previously acquired knowledge" (Christophersen, 1939, p. 72).

As Epstein (2002) notes, despite the divergences, most theories of the definite article have a lot in common: they focus primarily on one specific function of the definite article, namely the way it is used to pick out a discourse referent. They try to answer the question of what it is that allows one speaker to assume that a discourse referent will be identifiable (uniquely) or familiar to another speaker. The sources of definiteness that have been identified in the literature vary, and many terms have been used by different authors to capture the notion of definiteness: uniqueness, identifiability, unique identifiability, familiarity, inclusiveness, determinedness, individualization, concretization, actualization, specialization, particularization, salience (based on Epstein, 2002; Głaz, 2012; von Heusinger, n.d.).

Articles are often studied as one of the many semantic and discourse-pragmatic devices used in English for structuring information and maintaining topic continuity in discourse. The most widely cited and most influential typology of the sources of definiteness is to be found in the works of John Hawkins (1978, 1984, 1991). Firstly, Hawkins defines the "previous discourse set" – the entities that the interlocutors have talked about. For example, a

> mention of a professor permits subsequent reference to the professor. The speaker may have discussed numerous professors with other interlocutors and have entered them into the previous discourse sets that he shares with these individuals, he may be able to

access professors within the other kinds of pragmatic sets to be illustrated below, but as long as the previous discourse set shared with
the current interlocutor contains only one individual satisfying the
description professor, there will be no referential ambiguity through
non-uniqueness.

(J. A. Hawkins, 1991, p. 408)

Secondly, the

immediate situation of utterance in which the speaker and the hearer
find themselves can constitute a pragmatic set of entities for the purpose of uniqueness: Pass me the bucket will be unambiguous for the
hearer if there is just one bucket in his field of vision, irrespective of
the existence of countless buckets elsewhere.

(J. A. Hawkins, 1991, p. 408)

The third possibility is provided by what Hawkins calls a "larger situation set," that is, knowledge shared by people in the same physical
location, which explains why

inhabitants of the same town who have never met before can immediately talk about the mayor, meaning the unique mayor of their
town, and inhabitants of the same country can do likewise with the
president or the queen, despite the existence of numerous mayors,
presidents and queens elsewhere.

(J. A. Hawkins, 1991, p. 408)

Finally, there comes the most interesting source of definiteness in discourse, namely the general knowledge shared by speakers concerning "predictable co-occurrences of entities: (…) mention of a wedding permits immediate reference to the bride; a house sanctions the
roof; a car, the steering wheel; and so on" (J. A. Hawkins, 1991, p. 409).

Most semantic and pragmatic descriptions now recognize the above uses of the definite article. Labels often used for the above four uses are anaphoric, deictic, unique, and bridging (i.e., indirect) uses (von Heusinger, n.d.).

Definite and indefinite reference have long been a subject of study in the philosophy of language and in linguistic semantics (for an overview, see J. Lyons, 1977, pp. 179–187, or 1995, pp. 294–298). John Lyons points out the fact that the meaning of all referring expressions is context-dependent. A common noun preceded by a definite article may suffice without further description, even though the referent has not been previously mentioned, because the speaker can fairly assume in the given situation, that the hearer will know which of the potential referents satisfies the description he is referring to (J. Lyons, 1995, p. 181). Performing a definite description is an act of reference, in which the speakers "tacitly assure the addressee that the descriptive part of the expression will contain all the information that is required, in context, to identify the referent" (J. Lyons, 1995, p. 300).

2.6. CONCLUSIONS

At first sight, the place articles firmly hold in grammatical accounts of language use appears to be very much justified: they seem to form a system of oppositions and lend themselves to systemic descriptions, which aid learners of English to a certain extent. However, those descriptive accounts fail to reflect the full complexity of the English article system and to cover the entirety of existing and potential uses of the articles. Upon closer inspection, rules governing the use of articles turn out to be so complex and elusive that it remains something of a miracle that (most) language users end up using articles in a consistent fashion.

We have seen that articles are very common in English, that their distribution is connected not only with their syntactic role in a sentence, but that it also follows the information flow principle, which means that there is a strong pattern of the new information being indefinite and the given information – definite. Also, it was noted that some uses of articles, e.g. generic ones, are in fact less common in language than it may seem from descriptive approaches and pedagogical materials. (Pedagogical materials traditionally include an extensive discussion of generic uses.)

On the topic of definiteness, the following comment by Kambarov, even though it refers to natural language processing, seems to hold true for definiteness in language in general:

> a typical grammatical reference work addressing the concept of definiteness usually contains a large number of rules with numerous exceptions and special cases, which hinders effective use of information provided by determiners in nominal reference resolution.
>
> (2008, p. 1)

Definiteness is a much-studied and intriguing topic, but none of the theoretical treatments it has received so far have translated into clear rules which could be of pedagogical use.

Yet another source of considerable difficulty for learners of English is the notion of countability, due to the conceptual differences across languages as far as the count/non-count distinction is concerned. Finally, there are numerous instances where the use of the definite, indefinite or zero article is in contradiction to other rules which seemingly should apply, as, for example, in many expressions where the zero article is used with singular countable nouns.

CHAPTER 3

Other approaches to articles

3.1. INTRODUCTION

The first chapter of this book presented descriptive approaches to articles, while the second one looked at the key concepts behind the use of articles, most notably reference, definiteness and countability. It was shown that the philosophy of language and semantics have contributed to the understanding of these notions. This chapter provides a brief overview of some other important linguistic approaches to articles.

3.2. SOCIO-PRAGMATIC APPROACHES

One important development in the philosophy of language which has direct relevance to the study of articles is the work of Paul Grice. A closer look at instances involving the use of the definite article makes it clear that the instances of its use are not only dependent on the preceding text as such, but on general pragmatic knowledge, and on the situational context. Therefore, the motivation for the use of the definite article lies outside language as such. As is acknowledged in the *Longman Grammar*, "the interpretation of definite noun phrases often requires extensive pragmatic inferencing on the part of the addressee" (p. 264). In fact, making inferences is what the listeners do in order to preserve a sense of coherence in what they are told. This is the reason why traditional sentence-based semantics cannot fully account for many linguistic phenomena, including the use of articles. It is clear that an analysis of the use of articles cannot be complete without recourse to pragmatics.

The first theory that managed to account for inferencing was formulated by Grice as the principle of conversational implicature (Grice, 1975), which was later extended and developed into relevance theory by Sperber and Wilson (Sperber & Wilson, 1995). The Gricean maxims (Grice, 1975) of conversational cooperation (of quality, quantity, relevance, manner) explain why, in the following exchange:

> A: *Did you give Mary the money?*
> B: *I'm waiting for her right now.*

The inferred answer to A's question is negative. In the theory of relevance, the hearer's inferential strategy is motivated by a single principle of relevance, which holds that "Every act of ostensive communication communicates the presumption of its own optimal relevance" (Sperber & Wilson, 1995, p. 158).

A recent very interesting line of research on the English definite article is of socio-pragmatic character. Acton (2014), in an analysis rooted in Gricean pragmatics, looks at the English definite article and analyses how the definite article contributes to the social meaning of an utterance. For example, his corpus study shows that when referring to a group of people, using the definite article (e.g. "the Americans") instead of a bare plural ("Americans") presents the group as a homo-geneous entity of which the speaker is not a part (Acton, 2014).

3.3. COGNITIVE ACCOUNTS OF DEFINITE ARTICLE USE

As can be seen from the above overview, reference is a concept which is crucial to the understanding of how definite and indefinite arti-cles function in English. Cognitive linguistics has contributed sig-nificantly to providing a theory which elucidates many aspects of reference. It is now common (see Kambarov, 2008) to see referents of nouns in a text as elements of one of several alternating mental spaces, which provide "a level of conceptual organization between the text and reality" (Kambarov, 2008, p. 4). The specific theory within cog-nitive linguistics from which this concept arises is the Mental Spaces Theory (Fauconnier, 1994). It is a theory of dynamic meaning con-struction, the cornerstone of which is the proposition that discourse is divided into distinct mental spaces, which feature counterparts linked together by connectors. Mental spaces are set up to recruit temporary structure from the local discourse context and from other sources, including long-term memory. This process is known as "schema induction." As language users make sense of a text, they assign truth values to entities and relations between them in a given mental space, updating them on the basis of whatever information becomes availa-ble in the discourse, as well as on the basis of the existing knowledge they have, which is organized in hierarchical structures known as "frames." Existing mental spaces are altered to form new ones, which results in the creation of a mental spaces lattice.

As cognitive approaches to language typically seek to ground language description in general cognitive mechanisms, also in this case, the process of forming mental spaces is seen as governed by non-linguistic cognitive principles (Evans, 2007, pp. 135–136), and language is only a source of prompts which initiate this process. Since, as Fauconnier observed, language does not carry meaning, but guides it (1994, p. xxii), articles can be seen as signals which help the receiver to manipulate mental constructs containing referents of nouns.

A detailed cognitive account of the working of the English article system is provided by Epstein (e.g. Epstein, 2002), who drew on the work of Fauconnier (1994) and Ariel (1990). Epstein invokes a statement by Birner and Ward that "none of the previous analyses can account for all uses of the definite article in English" (Birner & Ward, 1994, p. 101) and argues that none of the approaches to defining definiteness are fully satisfactory. He points out that, because of its "enormous complexity" (Epstein, 2002, p. 338), indirect anaphora is very difficult to define in precise formal terms. Like Ariel and Fauconnier, Epstein considers grammatical elements in general to be discourse processing instructions. In this view, the basic meaning of *the* is to signal to the addressee the availability of an "access path." In other words, the definite article indicates that the knowledge required for interpreting a noun phrase is accessible (either already active or able to be activated) somewhere in the dynamic configuration of spaces. The use of the definite article signals to the recipient that there is a connection between the discourse entity and some other entity. The exact connection has to be worked out by the recipient, which explains why some utterances may be ambiguous (Epstein, 2002, pp. 334–346).

Epstein's account of article use is particularly convincing with respect to certain "strange" uses of the definite article which can be found especially in literary fiction and journalism, such as, for example, the use of *the* with first-mention nouns which are neither accompanied by any modification, nor can be assumed to be identifiable for the hearer. Epstein explains how the definite article in such contexts derives from prominence in subsequent discourse. For instance, it may signal the point of view of the narrator, or the protagonist. This can be illustrated with the following example from Epstein's paper, which is the opening sentence of Hemingway's *A Farewell to Arms*:

> In the late summer of that year we lived in a house in a village that looked across the river and the plain to the mountains.

According to Epstein, the passage encourages the reader to adopt the point of view of the narrator, by using the definite article with nouns that have not been mentioned before, and which cannot be assumed to be familiar or identifiable to the reader (the river, the plains, the mountains).

Another similar example comes from a newspaper:

> Sierra Madre resident Andy Dotson might not have needed to breach security barricades to return to his threatened home. He had forgotten his tattered, 19-year-old blanket with the distinctive penguin design. "The kids and the animals are my security blanket, they come first," he said. "But my family didn't get [the blanket], so I went back there. It means something to me. I was gonna bust through the barricades if I had to."
> (*Los Angeles Times*, 30 October 1993, p. A10, cited by Epstein, 2002,
> p. 365)

The definite article in *the distinctive penguin design* signals that the blanket is being described from the point of view of the man who went back into a building on fire in order to retrieve it.

Epstein also makes the very interesting point that the definite article signals a *low* level of accessibility to the referent. One of Epstein's examples is a comparison of the following two utterances (Epstein, 2002, p. 340):

a. *There's a cat in the yard. It's eating a mouse.*
b. *There's a cat in the yard. The cat is eating a mouse.*

There is no doubt that (a) is the more usual, natural of the two. The referents of both *it* and *the cat* are uniquely identifiable, as they have just been introduced. However, they remain highly accessible, because *a cat* is introduced in the first sentence, and there is no intervening discourse between the first and the second sentence. *The* is reserved for contexts with a lower degree of accessibility, this is why it seems unnatural in (b), where accessibility is high.

Another example from Epstein illustrates how speakers use the definite article with a referent that is new, so it is not yet identifiable to the interlocutor, but the speaker signals that he is intending for this to become the new topic of conversation, i.e., he assumes that the introduction will need elaboration on, and that the interlocutor knows it too (Epstein, 2002, p. 335):

> *M: Did you hear about the fight?*
> *A: What fight?*
> *M: Between Bob and Grandpa.*

In this account, the definite article emerges as essentially a discourse processing instruction,

> … signalling that the means for interpreting the NP in which it occurs is available somewhere in the configuration of mental spaces, as long as the appropriate spaces, elements and connections – i.e., access path – can be constructed by the addressee. Some of the functions fulfilled by *the* are: unique identifiability, prominence, role/value status, point-of-view shifts. Each function represents a conventional interpretation potentially associated with a definite description. However, none of these functions is specifically conveyed by the article itself. Instead, the interpretation of a given definite description arises in a particular context through a combination of lexical, grammatical, and pragmatic factors.
>
> (Epstein, 2002, p. 371)

Epstein's approach is useful in that it demonstrates that neither familiarity nor identifiability are sufficient conditions for determining definite article use. The mental spaces theory is very good at explaining some uses of the definite article which the previous theories could not account for, such as indicating the discourse prominence of an entity, the entity's status as a role function, or the fact that an entity is presented from a noncanonical point of view.

Another cognitive account of English articles has been put forward by Głaz (2012), whose work was inspired by Vantage Theory, a model of categorization developed by linguist and anthropologist Robert E. MacLaury, whose work concerned mostly colour categorization and the way it reflects the way humans orient themselves in space and time (MacLaury, 1995). Like Epstein, Głaz arrives at a plausible explanation of a number of uses of English articles which could not be accounted for in terms of reference, specificity or uniqueness. An introductory illustration of his approach is provided in the following excerpt, analysed in Głaz (2012), of the beginning of Doris Lessing's novel *The Good Terrorist*:

> The house was set back from the noisy main road in what seemed to be a rubbish tip. A large house. Solid. Black tiles stood at angles along the gutter...

In this excerpt, the house is first introduced with a definite article, then referred to again, this time with an indefinite article, which is the opposite of should be happening according to the "rule" of prior mention. The first sentence assumes familiarity with the house, while the second treats the house as merely a member of the category of houses. Drawing on vantage theory, Głaz models the conceptualization of the house as the succession of three vantages: recessive, dominant, and recessive again. In Głaz's opinion, applying Vantage Theory to the use of articles makes it possible to explain some seemingly arbitrary uses, usually considered to be motivated by convention only, by revealing the "cognitive motivation" behind them (Głaz, 2012, p. 18).

Recently, reference and definiteness have been studied in the context of natural language processing. In this field, reference is an important issue, as one of the main challenges in computerised processing of human language is co-reference resolution, that is, determining which words refer to the same entities (for example, anaphorically). The challenges in nominal reference resolution centre around identifying cases of co-reference, and instances of new entities being introduced into discourse. Kambarov (2008) has established a set of rules that "capture the factors essential to the concept of definiteness" in the form of an algorithm, the purpose of which is to aid the process of resolving reference in natural language processing. He proposes an algorithm for nominal reference resolution that uses the definiteness value of each determiner phrase to guide the search for its referent. This work is inspired by cognitive linguistics, as the author draws on the theory of mental spaces. The algorithm organizes referents of all encountered nouns in structures that correspond to mental spaces that are being described.

3.4. THE GENERATIVE TRADITION

What generative approaches have in common is that they do not treat articles as a word category in itself. Rather, like most descriptive grammars, they include them among the four categories of determiners, along with demonstratives (*this*), quantifiers (*many*, *three*), and possessives (*my*). A second assumption that most generative approaches share is that L2 acquisition does not start from scratch like in L1 development, but relies on the entire set of parametric values fixed in the L1; this assumption is known as the "full transfer hypothesis" (Schwartz & Sprouse, 1996). Consequently, the learning and processing of L2 articles would begin with the parametric values that the learners established for articles in their L1. In this view, L2 acquisition is a question of parameter resetting (see Kaltenbacher, 2001).

Beyond those two assumptions, the multiplicity of approaches in generative grammar and the various roles they assign to articles make it difficult to identify commonalities among them regarding the acquisition of L2 articles. Represented for a long time as mere specifiers of nouns inside Noun Phrases (NPs), determiners have been considered to play a more important role in some recent syntactical models, where they are perceived as heads of the phrases in which they appear. Those phrases are consequently labelled Determiner Phrases (DPs) rather than Noun Phrases (NPs) (see Hudson, 2004; Van Langendonck, 1994). Within the Determiner Phrase (DP), the determiner is one of a series of functional categories that head a maximal projection with abstract features such as [±definite], [±specific], [±count]. However, disagreement persists among theoreticians, and Granfeldt's statement that "there seems to be no consensus on the internal structure of the DP" (2000, p. 264) apparently still holds true.

Moreover, the fact that articles are morphemes raises further divergences. Some researchers agree with White's claim that "UG does not have anything to say about morpheme acquisition as such: morphemes are lexical items; they are language specific and have to be learned" (L. White, 1989, pp. 30–31). Other researchers in Generative Grammar (e.g. Vainikka & Young-Scholten, 1996) suggest that the L2 initially develops exclusively from the parametric values and syntactic projections of lexical items project, and that functional items such as articles only come into play at a later stage in L2 development.

In some languages, articles carry a limited information load, such as English, where they only indicate definiteness. In other languages, such as French or Spanish, they convey information about definiteness, number and gender.[6] Consequently, mastering an article system in a second language is challenging not only for speakers of article-less languages;[7] they also pose greater difficulty for learners whose L1 contains articles, in cases where those articles function differently from the L2, or – in generative terms – when the "parameter settings" differ across languages. Researchers have formulated various parameter-based hypotheses to explain the emergence or mastery of articles. A combination of two parameters is found in L2 studies on the acquisition of English articles: the [±specific referent] and the [±hearer knowledge] parameters. The former concerns whether the article and noun refer to a specific entity, and the latter concerns whether their referent is known to the hearer. This issue will be discussed in more detail in section 5.3.

3.5. CORPUS-BASED PERSPECTIVES

Corpora are covered here in this last section because, thanks to advances in technology, only recently has corpus-based research gained considerable ground and made notable advances. Apart from informing descriptive accounts of the article system (most notably the *Longman Grammar*), corpora also provide information on the distribution of articles across registers and on the frequency of their occurrence.

According to the *Longman Grammar*, the indefinite article appears with a frequency of approximately 20,000 per million words

---

6   The picture is further complicated by the fact that in some languages, such as classical Arabic, definiteness is conveyed by the article, while indefiniteness is conveyed by the noun (as is the case of English but only in the plural). In Swedish, it is the opposite situation: definiteness is conveyed by the noun, indefiniteness by the article.

7   One of the rare exceptions to that finding is Deprez, Sleeman and Guella (2011).

in the written registers (which amounts to 2% of the running text) and about 13,000 words per million in conversation (i.e., 1.3%). While the indefinite article is distributed in a more or less similar manner across registers, there is much greater variance in the distribution of the definite article. The definite article is very common in academic prose (with a frequency of ca. 55,000 per million words, i.e., 5.5%), fiction (ca. 42,000, which means 4.2% of all the words are definite articles), and is the least frequent in conversation, with only around 20,000 instances of use per million words (2%).

The lower frequencies of articles in conversation than in texts are caused, among other things, by the lower frequencies of nouns, and higher frequencies of proper names and personal pronouns. In conversation, the indefinite article with its function of introducing new entities is sometimes replaced by the demonstrative determiners *this/these*, but corpus analyses show that this use is predominantly restricted to informal spoken language.

According to the *Longman Grammar*, the definite article is the most frequent determiner of all. It occurs more often than its most popular "replacements," that is, other definite determiners, possessive and demonstrative ones. The proportion of the occurrences of the definite article with respect to other words that can appear in the same position varies across registers; the relative frequency of the definite article is the highest in academic prose.

The authors of the *Longman Grammar* observe that anaphoric reference is intuitively perceived as the most common use of the definite article. However, they note that when the definite article use is investigated in a corpus, other uses emerge as equally or even more common. In fact, anaphoric reference accounts for less than one third of the uses of definite noun phrases, while situational reference is surprisingly common. This observation resulted most likely from the inclusion of spoken language in the corpus under investigation.

There are also quite notable differences between registers. For example, situational uses account for 55% of cases in conversation, while they make up only 5% in the news or in academic sub-corpora. This is fully justified, because, as the authors say,

> conversation is embedded in a situation which is shared by the speaker and hearer. Moreover, conversational partners are usually closely related as family members or friends, and can thus rely on a great deal of shared knowledge.
>
> (*Longman Grammar*, p. 267)

Thinking of future research in this area, it is worth noting that, in their attempt to classify the uses of the definite article across a variety of registers, Biber and his colleagues (1999) were unable to classify (label: "uncertain") between 5 and 25% of the uses, depending on the register.

3.6. CONCLUSIONS

This chapter has looked at some of the theoretical approaches to articles and how their proponents attempt to make sense of the seemingly confusing character of the English article system. The above review provides only a very brief overview of the most important approaches, but it is enough to show that articles have received a considerable amount of attention from scholars representing various schools of linguistic thought. The fact that there exist such extensive treatments of various concepts relevant to the use of articles (for example, definiteness or specificity), brings home the fact that the issues involved are indeed very complex.

One approach which offers a very inspiring look at the English articles is cognitive linguistics. However, even though cognitive accounts of article use are fascinating, and they apparently cover a much wider range of article uses than competing accounts, providing insights into the conceptualisations behind article use, the explanatory power of this approach does not easily translate into practical applications. The explanations offered by cognitive linguists have an essentially post-hoc character. Also, even if some of its aspects could be used for teaching purposes, the intricacies of such concepts might be too complex to grasp for many practitioners.

CHAPTER 4

Articles as a source of difficulty in SLA

4.1. INTRODUCTION

When English is taught as a second language in an English-speaking country, that means, mostly to learners who are immigrants, teachers tend to be less aware of specific L1-induced areas of difficulty for their learners, due to the heterogeneity of the learners' L1 background. However, English is also taught in what is sometimes referred to as a "foreign language" context, in non-English speaking countries, which are sometimes very linguistically homogeneous, as is the case with Poland. In such contexts, teachers tend to be well aware of the typical problem areas to expect from their students, and it is common knowledge which target language features tend to cause difficulty. The English articles are a classic example of a well-known problem area, and it is also possible that some of the teachers themselves, being speakers of L1 Polish, might be less confident than usual when it comes to correcting their students' article errors.

Since the statement that "articles are difficult" is such a common remark in the English teaching context in Poland, this chapter provides an overview of theoretical perspectives on the concept of difficulty, to see if those theoretical perspectives allow for a better elucidation of the reasons which underlie the challenges posed by this specific feature of the English language.

4.2. THEORETICAL APPROACHES TO DIFFICULTY

A number of criteria have been put forward in the literature, in a rather chaotic and scattered matter, to account for what it means for a structure to be difficult, including formal or structural complexity, form-meaning relationships, developmental stages, learnability, typological markedness, and teachers' perceptions of learner difficulty (see Ekiert & Han, 2017). Difficulty has been described as a very challenging concept to define (see DeKeyser, 2005 for an in-depth discussion). According to Housen and Simoens, the existing literature on the topic is scarce,[8] difficulty is usually investigated in connection with a different concept which is the main focus of research, and

> the study of difficulty in SLA has been plagued with terminological difficulties, conceptual confusion, and misunderstandings of its relationship with other related yet conceptually distinct constructs such as linguistic complexity, learnability, and developmental stages and orders of acquisition.
>
> (2016, p. 164)[9]

---

[8]   However, one could point out that with respect to specific aspects of SLA, for example vocabulary, the concept of difficulty has been defined (see e.g. Nation's concept of learning burden (2001)) and investigations have been conducted to determine what constitutes difficulty (e.g. Laufer, 1997).

[9]   For a more comprehensive review of the situation, see Housen and Simoens (2016), also Ekiert and Han (2017).

Importantly for this discussion, many accounts of difficulty are entirely L2-centric, which means that they do not mention L1/L2 differences as a potential source of difficulty, which renders them inadequate for analysing the case of articles, since, as has already been mentioned and as will be made clear by the review of research in the next chapter, cross-linguistic differences play an important role in determining the level of difficulty for learners. In the days of contrastive analysis, articles were an ideal argument supporting the hypothesis that differences between the L1 and the L2 lead to difficulty with specific aspects of the L2. However, despite the predictive power of contrastive analysis when it comes to articles, the approach generally lost its popularity in the 1960s and 1970s, when generative grammar and cognitivism replaced behaviourism as theories informing approaches to the study of L2 acquisition (see Pichette & Leśniewska, 2018). Actually, Housen and Simoens (2016) suggest that difficulty was for a long time an unpopular topic of inquiry precisely because it was associated with contrastive analysis, which was considered outdated and insufficient (see Lightbown & Spada, 2006).

The concept of difficulty re-emerged in language studies near the turn of the century, partly due to the advent of available large language corpora, and in connection with studies of structural and formal complexity, which tend to be L2-centric. Formal complexity may be defined in many different ways, depending on which linguistic theory is applied, for example, it may be operationalized as the number of transformations needed to arrive at a certain construction. However, regardless of which linguistic theory is adopted by the researcher, the general rule is that the more "complicated" a construction is, the more difficult it is to learn and use. In this view, articles are not difficult at all, since they are formally very simple. Interestingly, Spada and Tomita (2010) use the example of articles to argue that structural complexity does not function as a predictor of difficulty, since structurally they are an example of the simplest structures possible, derived by one transformational rule, in contrast to more complex structures, which require a greater number of transformations.

4.2.1. DIFFICULTY AS COGNITIVE COMPLEXITY

Fortunately, a very recent publication by Housen and Simoens (2016) offers a useful taxonomy in which there is a place for L1-L2 differences, and which combines all the different approaches to difficulty into one framework. I will attempt to apply this framework for analysing the specific difficulty caused by articles. To avoid terminological confusion, Housen and Simoens propose to distinguish between structural complexity (or linguistic/absolute complexity), which means

> the inherent linguistic properties of a language feature or (sub)system (…) typically operationalized in terms of the number and variety of the discrete components of which a language feature consists,
>
> (2016, p. 166),

and cognitive complexity, which

> has to do with how costly, demanding, or difficult a given language feature is for a given language learner in a given learning context, particularly in terms of the mental resources allocated and cognitive mechanisms deployed in processing and internalizing the feature.
>
> (2016, p. 166)

It thus follows that structural complexity may be a contributing factor to cognitive complexity, but the two do not coincide. For the rest of this discussion, I shall adopt the terminology proposed by Housen and Simoens, with *difficulty* used to refer to cognitive complexity. Thus, "a language feature is more difficult than another if its processing and learning requires more time and/or more mental activity from a particular learner in a particular learning context" (2016, p. 166).

Within this framework, three main types of difficulty are recognized: feature-related difficulty (which is described as "objective"),

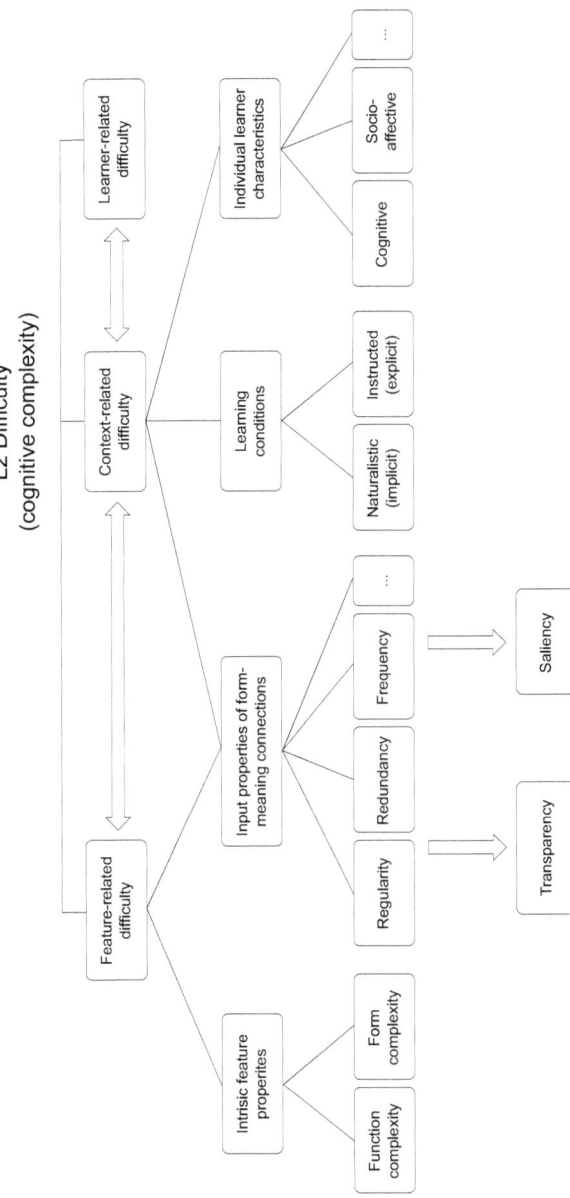

Figure 1. A taxonomy of learning difficulty offered by Housen and Simoens (2016).

context-related difficulty, and learner-related difficulty (described as "subjective"). An important characteristic of this framework is the recognition that all the main types and sub-types interact with one another (see Figure 1).

4.2.2. FEATURE-RELATED DIFFICULTY

A useful distinction made by the creators of this framework is that feature-related difficulty can be seen as resulting from two types of factors: firstly, feature-intrinsic properties, and secondly, the way in which this particular feature appears in the input. Feature-related complexity can be either formal or functional.

The intrinsic formal (structural) complexity can be assessed according to a variety of different linguistic theories, and the assessment of the degree of such complexity need not be exactly the same according to, for example, a generative, typological or a cognitive account of language. However, regardless of which theory is applied, the level of complexity is a feature of the specific structure in question, regardless of its distribution in the input, which is a separate criterion. Functional (also called *semantic*, or *conceptual*) complexity refers to the number and character of the meanings and functions expressed, and the mapping of forms and functions onto each other. This aspect is reminiscent of the "one to one principle" (Andersen, 1984), which postulates that the acquisition of a new form is greatly facilitated when there is a clear and unique correspondence between form and meaning. Input-related properties, in turn, such as regularity, redundancy, and frequency, all contribute to how transparent and how salient the feature will be to the learners. The more salient and transparent a feature appears to the learner, the easier it is to learn.

4.2.3. CONTEXT-RELATED DIFFICULTY

The second type of difficulty is determined by the context, that is, by the learning conditions. It is important to distinguish between naturalistic (or unguided) learning contexts, and instructed (or guided) ones. The former are said to encourage implicit processing, while the latter involve explicit attempts at guiding the learner's cognitive resources. This may involve "directing learners' cognitive resources to the targeted form-meaning mappings by enhancing their transparency, modifying their input frequency, or otherwise increasing their salience so that, ultimately, their learning difficulty is mitigated" (Housen & Simoens, 2016, p. 169). One more crucial role of instruction (apart from modifying or enhancing the presentation of form-meaning mappings in the structured input which is offered to the learners) is to provide learners with metalinguistic propositions, commonly known as grammar rules as instantiated in pedagogical books. Both the implicit-explicit distinction and the issue of metalinguistic propositions have important implications for the learning and use of articles, and they will be discussed in more depth in the sections which follow.

4.2.4. LEARNER-RELATED DIFFICULTY

The third type of difficulty is related to the learner, and, in this category, we finally find a place (though, admittedly, not a prominent one) for crosslinguistic aspects. The most important learner factors are "individual differences in cognitive abilities, particularly language aptitude (...), working memory, and implicit and procedural learning ability" (Housen & Simoens, 2016, p. 167), as well as socio-affective and personality factors, but there is also a place for "the learner's previous knowledge" which encompasses the first language or any other language already known by the learner. The learner-related factors also include overall L2 proficiency and stage of L2 development. Taken together, these learner differences are considered to be "the core ingredients of L2 learning difficulty" (Housen & Simoens, 2016, p. 167).

4.2.5. SOME FINAL WORDS ON OBJECTIVITY

Perhaps the most problematic element of this framework is the treatment of functional (semantic, conceptual) complexity as objective. All-feature related aspects of difficulty are believed to be "objective," because "some language features are more cognitively demanding for all language learners, irrespective of their individual learner characteristics" (Housen & Simoens, 2016, p. 167). Commonsensically, this is hard to accept, since even the most complicated form-meaning mapping in L2 will be relatively easy for certain learners if it happens to be very similar to the one in their L1.

To give a very simple example, beginners' courses in German for speakers of English usually devote a note or a section in one of the very first lessons on the German word *bitte*, because in German it is used with a number of meanings (situations) in which different English expressions would be used (though different intonations may accompany the different meanings of *bitte*):

Please (when asking for something, or asking someone to do something)
You're welcome (when responding to thanks)
Here you go (when handing something over)
May I help you? / What would you like? (from a person who wants to take your order)
Pardon? (when asking for a repetition)

Even though the difficulty here is minor, because the target form is a single, simple word, there is some remapping of form to meaning required; whereas for a Polish learner of German, this particular issue does not arise, as the Polish word "proszę" mostly overlaps with "bitte" in the range of situations in which it can be used.

The challenge one faces with trying to think of meaning-related difficulty as separate from crosslinguistic aspects can be illustrated with this passage from an article by DeKeyser:

> Linguistic difficulty is due to the characteristics of the L2 target: the meanings to be expressed, the forms used for expressing them, and most crucially, the form-meaning mappings. (…) Meanings can be difficult because they are both novel (not represented in L1) and abstract, and hence hard to infer from the input. The semantics of articles and of grammatical aspect marking on the verb are notorious examples of this. Classifiers in languages like Chinese, Japanese, or Korean are somewhat less abstract but are still novel for many learners; conversely, person, number, and tense marking on the verb are far from obvious for speakers of these languages.
>
> (DeKeyser, 2016, p. 354)

This passage strongly suggests that it is impossible to consider the difficulty of the "L2 target" without considering it through the lens of the L1 (or other languages the learner knows).

4.2.6. ARTICLES AND FEATURE-RELATED DIFFICULTY

However, assuming this problematic aspect can be overcome, the above framework can be used to assess the difficulty level of the English articles. First of all, articles score very low on form complexity, so in this sense they are easy. Their functional complexity, however, is high. In a taxonomy for assessing learning difficulty, Roehr-Brackin and her colleagues (Roehr & Gánem-Gutiérrez, 2009; Silva & Roehr-Brackin, 2016) distinguish between opacity of form-meaning mapping (one form, X meanings) and opacity of meaning-form mapping (one meaning, X forms). In the case of articles, it is the first of the two which is the source of difficulty, as each of the L2 forms (*the* and *a/an*) maps onto multiple meanings or functions (see also Shintani & Ellis, 2013). Additionally, one of the categories involved, the distinction between countable and uncountable nouns, is difficult in itself, because (like grammatical gender) it is not predictable (see 2.4).

As far as the input properties are concerned, articles are very frequent, which should contribute to noticing, and thus lower the level of difficulty. It is interesting to note here that this characteristic (high frequency) is a facilitating feature only when input properties are concerned. When it comes to language production, the situation looks radically different. As Master notes (2002: 332), in the case of articles, their high frequency adds a significant burden to the learner's language production, as it makes it necessary to continuously apply a set of complex rules. However, this view of frequency as a source of difficulty does not fit within the present framework, which is reception-oriented, and does not account for language production.

As far as articles are concerned, there is a characteristic which is missing from the framework under discussion and from most other sources which list difficulty-inducing factors. Among the input-related properties, an important difficulty-inducing factor which should be included is something that DeKeyser (2005) refers to as "optionality," and I will adopt this term. In his words:

> Optionality of certain elements, such as null subjects in Spanish or Italian (…) or case marking in Korean, only makes matters worse.

Not only does the optional character of the case marking or the overt subject pronoun suggest it is redundant, but its alternating presence or absence in the presence of the same meaning, except for subtle aspects of pragmatics, makes the form-meaning link even harder to establish.

(DeKeyser, 2005, p. 8)

Optionality is an important article-related characteristic. Examples abound, but let me illustrate this phenomenon with an example from the pilot phase of the study which is presented in Chapter 8 of this book, in which native speakers of English were asked to supply missing articles in the sentence:

Airbags are supposed to inflate automatically in case of collision.

The following corrections were made by the respondents, in roughly equal proportions:

*Airbags are supposed to inflate automatically in **the** case of collision.*
*Airbags are supposed to inflate automatically in case of **a** collision.*
*Airbags are supposed to inflate automatically in **the** case of **a** collision.*

This lack of consistency in article use, along with the complex form-meaning mappings, results in low transparency of the input, which is a factor predicted to raise the difficulty level. Another difficulty-inducing factor is communicative redundancy, which in the case of articles is high, as in many cases utterances deprived of articles would be understandable.

4.2.7. SALIENCE

An element which appears in the framework proposed by Housen and Simoens (as a consequence of various input properties), and which is often evoked in comments about the learning of the English articles, is salience. Generally speaking, salience refers to the ability of a stimulus to stand out from the rest (N. C. Ellis, 2016). Items which are salient are more likely to be noticed, cognitively processed, and learned, whereas linguistic forms of low salience are more difficult both to perceive and to learn (N. C. Ellis, 2006). Importantly for the case of articles, low salience can override high frequency (N. C. Ellis, 2016).

It is very commonplace to read that articles in English are not very salient, or do not appear salient to the learners. However, any discussion of the concept of salience[10] in the literature has to be treated with caution, as the term seems to be used with whatever meaning that comes to the writer's mind, and the available publications, instead of working towards establishing a shared definition and a usable taxonomy of different types of salience, appear to take delight in the fact that the term cannot be defined with any clarity; as illustrated, for example, by the introduction to the very recent book *Salience in Second Language Acquisition* (Gass, Spinner, & Behney, 2018). In fact, somewhat amusingly, the different meanings are so different from each other that it is possible to find both statements that articles in English are salient and that they are not salient – not because there is an actual difference of opinion between the writers, but because what seems to be meant by "salience" is completely different, as illustrated by the following two quotations:

> … the SLA literature has clearly shown that English articles are
> considered to be a nonsalient feature. They are not phonologically

---

[10]   Or saliency, with the two terms often being used as synonyms in the literature.

salient, and misuse of articles rarely leads to communication break-
down ...

(Sheen, 2007b, p. 262)

The L1 also provides a platform for expectations and, hence, salience. For example, a learner who does not expect articles by virtue
of not having them in their L1 will not expect them in L2. When the
learner encounters them in the L2, the unexpectedness of articles
creates a space for their salience.

(Gass et al., 2018)

Rather than list the different understandings of salience that can
be inferred from various sources (they are very numerous, and it
is unlikely that one could arrive at an exhaustive list), let us focus
on the two that are important for discussing articles. The first one
refers to the phonetic features of the item. For example, Goldschneider and DeKeyser (2005) measure the "perceptual salience" of an item
by looking at its phonetic substance (number of phones), syllabic-
ity, and total relative sonority. In their meta-analysis of morpheme
acquisition studies, they found that perceptual salience, thus defined,
was the best predictor of the sequence of acquisition for morphemes,
stronger than frequency or morphophonological regularity. It seems
that in this sense (understood in terms of phonetic qualities), salience would not be the outcome of various input-related properties,
as represented in the Housen and Simoens framework; rather, salience would be a combination of intrinsic features of the morpheme.

Goldschneider and DeKeyser (2005) thus measure perceptual salience by computing "the number of phones in the functor (phonetic
substance), the presence/absence of a vowel in the surface form (syl-
labicity), and the total relative sonority of the functor" (p. 48). When
compared to most words found in an English text, it becomes evident
that *the* and *a/an* possess fewer phones than most words, that they

contain only one syllable and vowel, and that as a consequence their total sonority (as calculated by the total number of points of each phone on the sonority hierarchy) is below average.

It should be noted that the salience of articles is even lower in spoken than in written language. Parrott makes the observation that because articles are pronounced in very weak form, learners may fail to notice them, and that learners who are exposed only to spoken English, but read relatively little, may be at a disadvantage when it comes to the acquisition of articles (Parrott, 2000, p. 50).

The other meaning of salience, which is often evoked in comments about the article system, seems to be more general, in the sense of "noticeable." This is, however, not really an objective characteristic of articles, but rather a combination of factors. As Nick Ellis explains (2016), ultimately salience depends not only on the features of the stimulus, but on the context and the learner. In this view, salience is ultimately in the eye of the beholder, as it is an outcome of certain expectations.

Statements of this kind – that articles are not salient in the sense of "noticeable" – are related to a number of observations made in the literature that articles tend to be overlooked by learners in the input. This is could be caused by both a lack of salience in the narrow, phonetic sense (e.g. Master, 2002), or to the fact that articles, like function words, tend to be overlooked when L2 learners process the language for meaning (Ekiert, 2004).

4.2.8. CONTEXT- AND LEARNER-RELATED DIFFICULTY

The middle section of the diagram in Figure 1 covers context-related aspects, that is, learning conditions, which may constitute yet another important source of difficulty. Although the graph provided by the creators of the framework does not indicate this, it seems reasonable to assume that the input-related properties mostly affect the naturalistic (implicit) mode of the two modes which we find under "learning conditions," whereas the feature-specific conditions affect the explicit mode, as they shape the metalinguistic descriptions of language rules. For implicit learning, the already-mentioned lack of transparency and low salience are predictors of difficulty. For explicit learning, the form-related aspects are relatively unproblematic, but the functional complexity of articles is high. Therefore, it comes as no surprise that the metalinguistic propositions (rule descriptions) used in the explicit teaching of article use are numerous and complicated. Another issue is how useful the propositions are and to what extent learners can profit from instruction, in other words, the question concerns the teachability of articles. This is an important issue, and will be taken up and examined in more detail later in this book. The implicit-explicit distinction is also important, and will be discussed later in this chapter.

Among individual learner characteristics, pride of place must go to the languages already known by the learner, as evidenced by the numerous studies which show that speakers of article-less languages have less success with article use (see section 5.2). Other learner characteristics are likely to play a role, but there is an apparent lack of studies that connect any specific individual learner differences with success in article use. Because some learners display persistent problems with articles, while other individuals apparently overcome this difficulty, it stands to reason that the ability to internalize the English article system is related to aptitude, which is a combination of different cognitive abilities which have been found to correlate with success in language learning (Carroll, 1981; Dörnyei & Skehan, 2003). To the best of my knowledge, the use of articles by L2 learners has not been investigated with respect to aptitude, which is not very surprising, given the limited number of studies on aptitude and language learning (see Yalçın & Spada, 2016 for a review).

However, we do know that certain subcomponents of aptitude correlate with success in learning specific features of a language. For example, in one study the success in learning the passive correlated with the component of grammatical inferencing, whereas the component of associative memory contributed to learners' gains on the past progressive (Yalçın & Spada, 2016). It would be very interesting to find out which of the components of language aptitude, if any, can be linked to success in using English articles by speakers of article-less L1s.

4.2.9. LANGUAGE PATTERNS VERSUS METALINGUISTIC PROPOSITIONS AND RULE DIFFICULTY

A number of comments have been formulated in the earlier chapters about the complexity of the "rules" that govern article use. To analyse this in more detail, one needs to take a closer look at what the rules are and consider the specific qualities that make them difficult. We should distinguish between different senses in which the term "rule" may be used. Though various such distinctions have been proposed (e.g. Dietz, 2002), for my present purposes the most useful appears to be a simple distinction between a) regularity in language (I will call it a "pattern"), and b) the description of such a pattern which attempts to capture that regularity by means of a metalinguistic description. Within the second category, various descriptions are offered within the frameworks of different linguistic theories, for example structural, generative, functional or cognitive. Among the many different linguistic descriptions, there is a special sub-category of descriptions that are typically pedagogical, aimed at L2 learners. These pedagogical rules may be based on any linguistic theory; however, most pedagogical grammars rely on descriptive grammars (R. Ellis, 2006). Understandably, pedagogical rules are usually simplified when compared to full descriptive accounts of a given language feature. As Housen and Simoens note, pedagogical rules may be very different from the actual target language features which they are attempting to describe, as they often are "perceived or intuited 'rule-like' patterns of covariance in the input" (Housen & Simoens, 2016, p. 169), and the same pattern may have very different metalinguistic descriptions.

Although rules and the reality can be presented as separate entities, and despite the usefulness of distinguishing between the pedagogical rules and the actual reality of the language that such rules try to capture, there must be some degree of correspondence between the level of complication of one and the other. It would be unusual to encounter an exceedingly complicated metalinguistic proposition delineating the rules for the use of the third person singular –*s* ending in English verbs in the present simple tense. The pattern is simple and works without exceptions. In contrast, a set of metalinguistic propositions explaining how to form conditional sentences, no matter how concise, must be more extensive.

In some studies, the distinction between a "rule" as a pattern in language, and a "rule" as a metalinguistic proposition is not implemented. For example, in a study by Scheffler (2011), "rule difficulty" (that the teachers in the study were supposed to rate) is a label that encompasses the structural and functional complexity of a grammatical pattern, as well as the difficulty of the pedagogical rule as such (the metalinguistic proposition in itself). No distinction is made between the two, which makes sense because the study aims at assessing teachers' judgment of rule difficulty, and it is quite likely that in teachers' and students' minds, the two are conflated. However, for the purpose of analysing the difficulty of the article system, the distinction between the actual language patterns and the linguistic descriptions of those is crucial, because there appears to be less overlap between one and the other in the case of articles than in the case of most syntactic patterns. I will therefore retain the distinction between language patterns and metalinguistic propositions in the discussion that follows.

4.3. IMPLICIT VERSUS EXPLICIT LEARNING AND KNOWLEDGE

Rod Ellis argues that "what constitutes learning difficulty needs to be considered separately for implicit and explicit knowledge" (2008, p. 4). The terms "explicit" and "implicit" have been used in SLA research for more than 35 years,[11] and many studies are based on the assumption that "explicit and implicit knowledge of language are represented differently and that explicit and implicit learning of language involve distinct cognitive processes" (Silva & Roehr-Brackin, 2016, p. 318).

The core meaning of the implicit-explicit distinction appears to revolve around the presence or absence of awareness (Andringa & Rebuschat, 2015; Hulstijn, 2005). Explicit learning, is "characterized by the learner's conscious and deliberate attempt to master some material or solve a problem" (Dörnyei, 2009, p. 136). It has also been defined as "learning to think and talk about the language system in symbolic terms – in terms of rules and their exceptions – by committing these to memory through practice and rehearsal" (Andringa & Rebuschat, 2015, p. 188). The learners may be presented with explicit rules which explain how a particular language feature works, or they may themselves form hypothetical rules on the basis of available evidence, but if they do it consciously, it also constitutes explicit learning. Explicit learning logically leads to explicit knowledge, which is also often described as the kind of knowledge that can be called

---

[11]   The distinction is related to, and can be seen as going back to, Stephen Krashen's "learning" versus "acquisition" dichotomy (see DeKeyser, 2003).

up on demand or articulated in a verbal statement (Silva & Roehr-Brackin, 2016).

Implicit knowledge, in turn, is usually described as intuitive, and one that cannot be brought into awareness or articulated (Dörnyei, 2009; Hulstijn, 2005). That type of knowledge seems to derive from implicit learning, which DeKeyser defines as "learning without awareness of what is being learned" (2003, p. 314). Whereas drawing on explicit learning is considered to be effortful, implicit knowledge is often associated with automatic processing (Hulstijn, 2005).

It has to be noted that the distinction between explicit and implicit knowledge, and explicit and implicit learning, though accepted by many scholars, is not universally recognized as valid. It also generates disagreement between researchers when those notions are analysed in finer detail.[12] Explicit learning involves a number of different constructs, which are themselves challenging and complicated to investigate, such as awareness, attention and noticing (see Leow, 2015). Many controversies remain as to the exact nature of implicit learning (see Godfroid, 2016 for a review).

It has been argued that implicit learning results from an unconscious, automatic, frequency-based process of induction (N. C. Ellis, 2005). N. C. Ellis gives the following extensive description of implicit learning:

(T)he bulk of language acquisition is implicit learning from usage. Most knowledge is tacit knowledge; most learning is implicit; the vast majority of our cognitive processing is unconscious. Implicit learning supplies a distributional analysis of the problem space: Frequency of usage determines availability of representation according to the power law of learning, and this process tallies the likelihoods

---

12   For a review of those issues, see DeKeyser (2003).

of occurrence of constructions and the relative probabilities of their mappings between aspects of form and interpretations, with generalizations arising from conspiracies of memorized utterances collaborating in productive schematic linguistic constructions. (…) Implicit learning also forges serial associations, synthesizing collocations, larger formulas, and composite constructions by chunking together contiguous components, thus creating hierarchical organizational structures. (…) Once associated, the components stimulate each other, via these connections, in the spreading activation of the cognitive unconscious. Related exemplars thus work together in implicit memory, their likenesses harmonizing into an attractor state, and it is by these means that linguistic prototypes and categories emerge. (…) Implicit learning, operating throughout primary and secondary neocortical sensory and motor areas, collates the evidence of language, and the results of this tallying provide an optimal solution to the problem space of form-function mappings and their contextualized use. The representational systems modularize over thousands of hours on task. In these ways, unconscious learning processes, which occur automatically during language usage, are necessary in developing the rationality of fluency.

(N. C. Ellis, 2005, pp. 306–307)

However, one should note that implicit learning has its limitations, since it exploits resources other than those involves in explicit earning, especially in relation to metacognition (Dienes & Perner, 2002). To that effect, Nick Ellis mentions in the same source that "many aspects of a second language are unlearnable – or at best are acquired very slowly – from implicit processes alone" (N. C. Ellis, 2005, p. 307). Unfortunately, the author does not provide information as to which aspects of SLA are alluded to by that remark.

The view that learning is unconscious, automatic, and frequency-based is consistent with the position which holds that the primary language learning mechanism is statistical learning (Rebuschat & Williams, 2012; Romberg & Saffran, 2010), which can be defined as "a gradual process of accumulating linguistic knowledge based on the distributional properties of the input" (Andringa & Rebuschat, 2015, p. 188). In this view, humans are sensitive to frequencies of (co-)occurrence, and, without being consciously aware of it, they accumulate this frequency information until patterns of grammatical structure emerge. This phenomenon is of central importance to phraseological aspects of language learning, which will be discussed in Chapter 7.

Even if most learning is indeed implicit, for the learning of specific L2 features over a limited period of time, explicit instruction is by far more efficient. De Keyser (2003) provides a review of studies which directly compared explicit and implicit instruction (the latter may involve input flooding, or presenting learners with a large amount of input containing the target pattern). Those studies, conducted in the form of experiments with artificial languages, as well as classroom experiments, invariably show that the explicit instruction groups strongly outperform implicit groups. This confirms the status of metalinguistic instruction as an invaluable way to speed up the learning process.

However, it is believed that, as opposed to the use of implicit knowledge, which is automatic and effortless, the use of explicit knowledge, i.e., relying on the conscious application of explicit rules in language comprehension and production, must be more cognitively demanding for the language user, as it taxes working memory resources (Silva & Roehr-Brackin, 2016). Therefore, it would be ideal if the learner could move beyond explicit knowledge to the faster, effortless implicit knowledge. In other words, hopefully the development of explicit knowledge in an L2 learner is not the final state, an end in itself, but an aid in the development of implicit knowledge. This brings us to an issue of crucial importance, namely, the relationship between implicit and explicit learning and knowledge. Does explicit knowledge help in the formation of implicit knowledge? Anyone involved in either learning or teaching an L2 must certainly hope that it does, otherwise the prospects for instructed L2 learning would be rather bleak: instructed learners would forever have to rely on the effortful process of applying explicit rules (which are never entirely accurate) when producing language output.

This pessimistic view, known in the literature as the no-interface position,[13] is generally considered unlikely (see e.g. Andringa & Rebuschat, 2015 for an overview), especially as it goes contrary to the bulk of research on automaticity that has been carried out with respect to language since the late 1970s. For example, Segalowitz interpreted neurophysiological evidence "to mean that explicit knowledge forms a prerequisite for implicit knowledge to come into existence" (2005, p. 378) and conducted a review of studies which suggest that "already in the initial phases of learning, implicit knowledge is spontaneously formed, and that explicit processes are simply not used any longer in the later phases" (2005, p. 378).

The discussion centres instead on which of the two other views, known as the strong- and weak-interface positions, is true. The former holds that explicit knowledge can turn into implicit knowledge as the result of practice; in the latter view, this is possible only to some extent, or under some conditions. Explicit instruction and metalinguistic information can be seen as a way of building up the target associations faster, a kind of shortcut to achieving a structure which would take much longer to emerge from the statistical learning process. DeKeyser's view, for example, is that explicit knowledge can become so automated with time and practice that it becomes impossible to distinguish it from implicit knowledge. Also, he points out that some learners, as a result of rule automatization and extensive

---

[13] The no-interface position can be seen (DeKeyser, 2003) as a continuation of Krashen's view that "learned competence does not become acquired competence" (Krashen, 1985, p. 42).

communicative use, may gradually lose their awareness of the explicit rules they once held in memory (DeKeyser, 2003). A weaker position is supported by Nick Ellis, who sees explicit instruction as a way to direct attention towards particular formal features of the input, which in turn affects the statistical, frequency-based uptake of those features (N. C. Ellis, 2015).

Another consideration which is important for the present discussion is the fact that no linguistic description, and – even more so – no pedagogical rule (because they have to be simple) can fully capture or depict the language patterns which they try to describe. However, I would argue that some language features are "depictable" (for lack of a better term). This "depictability" is low in the case of articles, as evidenced by the multiplicity of metalinguistic propositions needed to describe the way they are used, the numerous exceptions, and a fair amount of optionality.

To take this thought further, the easily "depictable" language patterns are the ones for which there is extensive (maybe even complete?) overlap between the language pattern and the explicit rule. It stands to reason that in such cases, highly proceduralized explicit knowledge may be virtually impossible to distinguish, in a learner's performance, from implicit knowledge. However, with poorly "depictable" patterns – such as the English articles – even a highly proceduralized knowledge of an extensive list of rules will not result in article use that is comparable to native speaker use.

This fact can be explained by differences in the nature of explicit and implicit knowledge. Certain inherent qualities of explicit and implicit knowledge make them a better match for some linguistic patterns and not for others. We find a pertinent observation on this topic in a publication by Roehr-Brackin:

> ... it has been argued that explicit knowledge is characterized by stable, discrete, and context-independent category structure.

Correspondingly, linguistic constructions which show comparatively systematic, stable, and context-independent usage patterns
can be described more easily by means of metalinguistic rules. Such
linguistic constructions should be more amenable to explicit learning
than linguistic constructions with less systematic and more context-
-dependent usage patterns that require a greater number of, or more
complex metalinguistic rules to describe them adequately.

(Roehr-Brackin, 2015, p. 126)

Thinking of English articles, this implies they are less amenable
to explicit learning, as they require a great number of metalinguistic
rules. They are more likely to be successfully used if learnt implicitly,
as "implicit representations with flexible, context-dependent category structure can fully capture prototype effects and distributional
effects" (Silva & Roehr-Brackin, 2016, p. 319), so they result in knowledge that is both reliable and accurate.

4.4. CONCLUSIONS

There are three main conclusions which emerge if the theoretical
considerations on difficulty in SLA presented in the above review
of literature are applied to the specific characteristics of the English
article system.

4.4.1. HIGH DIFFICULTY LEVEL

The first conclusion is that both implicit and explicit learning of articles is highly difficult. An examination, from a theoretical perspective, of the degree of difficulty posed by the article system in the

learning of L2 English, as presented in this chapter, confirms that there are indeed very sound reasons to regard the difficulty level as high.

Three main factors contribute to the difficulty posed by articles. Two of these are feature-related characteristics that have a negative impact on implicit learning. The first element is intrinsic to the articles themselves: Despite the fact that English articles are of low formal complexity, their functional complexity is high, which leads to high form-function opacity (one form may serve many functions). The second element is related to language input: despite their high frequency, articles are characterized by communicative redundancy and optionality, which means that articles are seldom needed to ensure understanding and sometimes more than one option is acceptable in the same context.

The combination of form-function opacity and optionality contributes to low transparency for articles, while their morpho-phonological composition, communicative redundancy, and optionality contribute to their low salience.

The third factor that makes articles difficult to master is especially relevant for explicit learning. Grammar books and pedagogical manuals contain a wealth of highly difficult descriptions to account for how English articles work (metalinguistic propositions), mostly due to a multiplicity of rules that govern article use.

4.4.2. IMPLICIT LEARNING

The second conclusion is that articles have to be learned implicitly. Due to the fact that article use is not well "capturable" by means of metalinguistic propositions, the explicit knowledge of article use (even highly proceduralized) does not enable the learner to use articles in a fully target-like way. Therefore, articles have to be learned implicitly to make the use fully native-like, even though this process is difficult, as was just stated in the first conclusion.

Another reason that the knowledge of article use must be highly automatized is related to frequency. Articles are very frequent in the input, which normally lowers the difficulty level for acquisition. However, their frequency brings about difficulties in the production of L2 utterances: consistent rule application, given that the rules are very complicated, is effortful and puts a strain on the learner's cognitive resources.

4.4.3. LIMITED USEFULNESS OF METALINGUISTIC PROPOSITIONS

The third conclusion is that metalinguistic rules show little promise for the teaching of articles. Chapter 6 will look at specific research findings concerning the teaching of articles. However, this chapter allows us to make some predictions on this topic. On the basis of theoretical considerations only, it seems that the chances of learning to use articles in a completely target-like manner as the result of explicit instruction are not very high, not because explicit instruction is generally ineffective (as was mentioned above, it has proven effective) but because articles do not lend themselves easily to explicit instruction. This indeed seems to be the prevailing view among language teachers. For example, Sheen (in a study which will be discussed later in this book) gives the following description of the situation in ESL classes at an American college:

> … a series of discussions with the participating faculty members at the college (…) revealed that (a) participating students are not explicitly taught articles during the semester, and (b) articles, though constituting a structure where students commonly make errors, are infrequently corrected because they are nonsalient and they require complicated rule explanations.
>
> (Sheen, 2007b, p. 262)

However, as was said above, explicit rules are valuable and time-saving in instructional settings. If they are of somewhat limited use as far as articles go, and fully implicit learning of the articles is not realistic given the time constraints of L2 learning[14] (no input flood has a chance of making a difference to the learner's implicit knowledge), it appears that the only potential for helping learners resides in exploring the possibility of awareness raising. Noticing tends to be hindered by the relatively non-salient character of articles and, as suggested by Yoo (2009), articles have suffered as a result of communicative approaches to language teaching, which emphasise fluency over accuracy. Encouraging noticing may lead to some improvement of the normally very slow processes of implicit learning.

---

[14] And given possible age effects, as there is also the possibility that implicit learning, even with a sufficient amount of input, may be constrained by maturational constraints (see DeKeyser, 2003); but it needs to be remembered that the specific nature and extent of maturational constraints is a matter of much controversy (see Muñoz & Singleton, 2011). At this moment there seems to be no reliable information regarding how age impacts the capacity for implicit vs explicit learning (see Andringa & Rebuschat, 2015; DeKeyser, 2003; Verneau, van der Kamp, Savelsbergh, & de Looze, 2014).

CHAPTER 5

Articles in SLA research

5.1. INTRODUCTION

In view of the immense complexity of the English article system, as well as its high level of difficulty, as discussed in the preceding chapters, the challenge facing learners of English as a second language seems considerable. The previous chapter has shown the numerous reasons why articles may cause difficulty for ESL learners, especially for those whose L1 contains no articles. As has already been mentioned, research findings confirm the significant difficulties that learners encounter with articles, but also provide information on other aspects of article acquisition and use. The overview below provides the most important facts about articles in L2 acquisition that have been established by researchers.

It should be noted here that information about the acquisition and use of articles is available from studies with a wide range of research topics, since any study dealing with learner language may gather information on the learners' use of articles, among many other language features. This makes it impossible to consider every single study which mentions articles, and the review of literature presented in this chapter is necessarily selective, discussing mostly studies which are concerned primarily with articles, but also selected ones in which articles were not the main focus of inquiry.

5.2. CROSSLINGUISTIC ASPECTS

From the vast body of research on articles, the finding about articles in L2 English which emerges with by far the greatest robustness and clarity is the observation that learners who do not have an article system in their L1 find it more difficult to acquire articles in an L2. The first observations about the crosslinguistic effects of learners' article use were made already in the early days of second language acquisition research. An important paradigm in the emerging field of applied linguistics, derived from Bloomfieldian linguistics, was that of contrastive analysis. Its basic assumption was that areas of difficulty in language learning can be identified and anticipated for speakers of a specific L1 on the basis of a comparison of the learner's language with the target language. The more different the rules were, the more problematic their learning was expected to be in an L2. It is not surprising that crosslinguistic aspects of the use of articles attracted considerable interest, since this topic was perfectly suited for contrastive analysis and the other dominant approaches of the day, error analysis and transfer studies. In one of the early studies on articles in a crosslinguistic context, Dušková (1969) attributed the article errors of Czech learners of English to the absence of articles in Czech. Polish linguists were among the first ones to publish observations on the problems caused by articles in the process of learning English by speakers of an article-less L1 (Arabski, 1968, 1990; Kałuża, 1963); it appears that already in the early days of English language instruction in Poland it was a recognized fact that "since articles do not exist in Polish, learners misuse them in many possible ways" (Arabski, 1968, p. 84).

The topic seems to have attracted less interest in the following decades, but evidence continued to accumulate on the importance of crosslinguistic factors in article acquisition and use. Larsen-Freeman, in a study of morpheme acquisition orders (1975), found out that the rank occupied by articles in morpheme accuracy studies was lower for speakers of article-less languages (e.g. Japanese) than for speakers of L1 that contain articles. A number of studies on Swedish and Finnish learners (reviewed by Ringbom, 1985) showed that Swedes, whose L1 has articles, make fewer errors than Finns, whose L1 does not have them.

More recently, a very interesting study by Jarvis (2002) yielded overwhelming evidence supporting the hypothesis that the use of articles in L2 is influenced by the article system of the L1. The study design involved eliciting narratives in English from native speakers of American English, Swedish, and Finnish. The Swedes and the Finns additionally wrote the same narratives in their L1. The author commented that, in terms of article use, the English texts written by Americans and Swedes "are, in fact, so conspicuously similar that they leave little doubt concerning the (facilitating) influence of L1 Swedish in this area of interlanguage performance" (Jarvis, 2002, p. 401). The Finnish data show a striking underuse of articles, and also points to the possibility of L3 influence, because those speakers of L1 Finnish who also studied Swedish displayed some advantage over non-Swedish-speaking Finns.

Success in article use is thus proven to be strongly dependent on crosslinguistic factors, with speakers of article-less languages finding English articles much more problematic than speakers of languages which feature independent prenominal article-like morphemes, who profit from facilitative effects of crosslinguistic similarity (Chrabaszcz & Jiang, 2014; R. Hawkins et al., 2006; Ionin, Zubizarreta,

& Maldonado, 2008; Snape, 2008; Zdorenko & Paradis, 2008).[15] This is in keeping with the growing recognition of the ubiquitous character of crosslinguistic factors in contemporary second language acquisition studies (Arabski & Wojtaszek, 2016).

5.3. SEMANTIC UNIVERSALS AND THE ACQUISITION OF ARTICLES

While there is plenty of evidence that speakers of languages which do not feature articles have greater difficulty learning how to use them in English, it is less clear how exactly that difficulty is to be accounted for in theoretical terms. The simplest approach would be to think that the semantic and discoursal roles played by articles (the marking of specificity and assumed hearer knowledge, the latter overlapping with the discoursal reference to new or reintroduced referents) are unknown to the language learner with an article-less L1. The learner has to learn new semantic and discourse knowledge, instead of just mapping a new form onto a meaning that is already known from the L1 (as in, for example, the past tense marking). However, this would be an oversimplification, as it is true that (as was mentioned above in the section on information flow) referentiality and definiteness are also known in article-less languages, at least to some extent. However, they are expressed through linguistic means so different that they are not normally apparent to language users (see e.g. Firbas, 1992).

---

[15] Even so, the acquisition of the English article system is not entirely unproblematic for speakers of languages which feature articles, as there are always some differences in article use between languages. For example, the French language has no zero-article, but it has an additional category of articles called partitives, which have no equivalent in English.

Despite there being a number of approaches to definiteness, as was shown in Chapter 2, and the semantics of articles being the subject of much ongoing discussion, the bulk of L2 acquisition studies on articles is almost entirely based on one particular model of the semantics of articles, stemming from the work of Bickerton (1981) and Huebner (Huebner, 1983). Bickerton (1981), in his *Language bioprogram hypothesis*, adopts an innateness perspective on article acquisition, which assumes that certain distinctions made in the selection of articles could be biologically programmed. He postulates the existence of two universals, or "primes": a semantic one, differentiating between a specific referent [+SR] and a nonspecific referent [–SR], and a discourse universal, differentiating between what he called "presupposedness" and "nonpresupposedness," that is, referents that are assumed to be known to the hearer [+HK] and referents assumed to be unknown to the hearer [–HK]. There are thus four possibilities for NP reference.

These four possibilities were presented by Huebner (Huebner, 1983, p. 133) in the form of a semantic wheel (see Figure 2), an illustration of the way these four combinations of universals are mapped onto article use in English:

- *the* for [+SR,+HK],
- *a* or Ø for [+SR,–HK],
- *a* or Ø for [–SR,–HK],
- *the*, *a*, or Ø for [–SR,+HK], that is, generic reference.

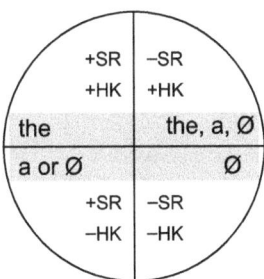

Figure 2. Huebner's (1983) semantic wheel.

A vast majority of studies on articles are based on Bickerton's conceptualization of NP reference and discourse function, or subsequent developments of that conceptualization (e.g. Chaudron & Parker, 1990; Díez-Bedmar & Papp, 2008; Tarone & Parrish, 1988). Those articles uses which fall outside of the semantic wheel were labelled by subsequent researchers as "idiomatic uses" (Butler, 2002; Thomas, 1989). This fifth category of article use includes expressions such as "in the 1970s," "all of a sudden" and "living hand to mouth," and contains all three article choices: *the*, *a*, and Ø.

A typical taxonomy used in research on ESL articles is presented in Table 1; it is a shortened version of the classification used by Díez-Bedmar and Papp (2008), who adapted it from earlier researchers (Butler, 2002; Ekiert, 2004; Huebner, 1985; Thomas, 1989). Most studies that look into selected, specific features of NP reference follow this taxonomy and thus focus on learners' sensitivity to the features of definiteness and specificity.

Features	Environment	Articles	Examples
Type 1 [−SR,+HK]	generic nouns	*a, the*, Ø	An elephant never forgets.
			They say that the elephant never forgets.
			Elephants have trunks.
Type 2 [+SR,+HK],	referential definites previous mentions specified by entailment or definition unique in all contexts / in a given context	*the*	Pass me the pen.
			I found a book. The book was ...
			The first person to walk on the moon...
Type 3 [+SR,−HK]	referential indefinites first-mention nouns	*a*, Ø	A man phoned.
			I keep sending messages to him.

Features	Environment	Articles	Examples
Type 4 [–SR,–HK]	non-referential nouns attributive indefinites non-specific indefinites	*a*, Ø	Alice is an accountant. I need a new car. Foreigners would come up with a better solution.
Type 5	idioms and conventional uses	*a, the*, Ø	all of a sudden, in the 1950s, living hand to mouth

Table 1. A typical taxonomy used in research on ESL articles (based on Díez-Bedmar & Papp, 2008).

The central question in this kind of research is whether the learners seem to have an innate – and therefore universal – sensitivity to certain semantic, syntactic, and discourse distinctions and, if so, how and when they mark such distinctions. The rationale behind investigating "universals" is the assumption that all languages have means of indicating reference, achieving topic continuity, and thus making sense of connected discourse. The marking of specificity and hearer knowledge may be present in other languages, even though they may be realized in other ways than through articles. Thus, on a general level, all learners of English "know" the function of the article system, as it is an alleged part of the Universal Grammar. They will, therefore, tend to mark it in one way or another, possibly using different formal means than native speakers of English. For example, researchers may be interested in whether, at the beginning stages of ESL learning, the functions of the article system are realized in interlanguage by means of other features transferred from the L1, for example, as hypothesized in the functional sentence perspective (Firbas, 1992), which requires that new information be positioned toward the end of the sentence.

As was mentioned in section 3.4, in generative studies, the acquisition of a new article system by language learners is seen as a process of parameter resetting. Various parameter-based hypotheses have been put forward to explain the mastery of articles, or persistent problems with this language feature. Providing an overview of such studies, Roger Hawkins (2001) offers a syntactical explanation of that definite-then-indefinite sequence in terms of complement specification and co-indexation for both article categories, denying any notable impact of the learner's L1 on the observed sequence of emergence in L2 English. However, some other researchers in Generative Grammar do acknowledge the impact of the learner's L1 when they interpret their results. Among those, Ionin, Ko & Wexler (2004) suggest their "fluctuation hypothesis," where the binary parameter for articles is definiteness/specificity. They argue that languages like English possess an article system based on definiteness, whereas in other languages, like Samoan, it is based on specificity.[16] Therefore, a learner of English whose L1 is French (also based on definiteness) would benefit from assigning the [+definite] to English, while a learner whose L1 contains no articles – such as Polish – would fluctuate for a certain amount of time between definiteness and specificity, thus mixing more *a/an* and *the* and producing a higher number of omitted articles (see Zdorenko & Paradis, 2008).

The fluctuation hypothesis was supported by Ionin, Ko & Wexler's study (2004). The authors gave a multiple-choice task to Korean and Russian learners of English, in which the learners were expected to choose one of the three possibilities (a, the, zero) in a given slot.

---

[16] For example, in English the definite article can be used even when referring to a specific entity (as was discussed in section 1.3). For example, it is possible to say "I want to talk to **the** manager" without knowing who that person is. In Samoan, the article would vary depending on whether the article refers or not to a specific entity.

Accuracy in the use of articles was better when definiteness and specificity had the same value. In other words, the [+definite, +specific] and [−definite, −specific] contexts yielded the highest accuracy rates. The options were available only with singular nouns. The learners were less successful with items which were [+definite, −specific] or [−definite, +specific]. The authors interpreted this to mean that the learners had yet to settle on the feature of definiteness. Similarly, Ionin, Zubizarreta, and Maldonado (2008) obtained results supporting the fluctuation hypothesis. Such fluctuation was also found by Zdorenko and Paradis (2008), whose child participants from both types of L1s (with and without articles) used both the definite and the indefinite article for the [−definite, +specific] context.

5.4. THE SEQUENCE OF ACQUISITION OF ARTICLES IN L1 AND L2 ENGLISH

The acquisition of articles in L1 English is, in contrast to the L2 situation, relatively unproblematic, although it takes some time to develop. Brown (1973) was the first to point out that articles are not very simple to master in comparison to other grammatical morphemes, since they ranked 8th out of the 14 morphemes he examined for the three children whose first language acquisition he followed. This means that articles appear in children's speech even after irregular past endings and the possessive *'s*. Subsequent studies investigating the order of acquisition of grammatical morphemes have confirmed that articles tend to be acquired quite late in comparison to other morphemes (for an overview, see Pawlak, 2006, pp. 103–107). Regarding the moment they become mastered, Warden (1976) showed that, at the age of three, children still use the definite article about half the time to introduce a noun in telling a story, instead of an indefinite article, which adults would use. The bulk of research conducted since then suggests that children seem to acquire the article system somewhere between 2;8 and 3;8 years of age, at which time they hardly make any article errors. If there are errors, it is mostly the overuse of the definite article when the hearer does not in fact have any knowledge of the referent (i.e., the [+SR, −HR] case), but they tend not to make errors when the referent is nonspecific and assumed unknown to the hearer, that is, in the [−SR, −HK] case (Brown, 1973; Maratsos, 1976).

This seems to make sense – children may not yet be able to make correct assumptions about the listener's knowledge, as this ability develops with experience and knowledge of the surrounding world. They do, however, seem to distinguish without any difficulty between specificity and nonspecificity, even though there are no physical features of the referents that make them specific or nonspecific as such (Maratsos, 1976, p. 94). It has been suggested that children have an innate sensitivity to specificity and nonspecificity, as assumed by Bickerton's (1981) bioprogram hypothesis.

According to a synthesis of studies on article acquisition in L1 (Cziko, 1986), four stages of this process can be distinguished:

- at Stage 1, all referential nouns, both [+HK] and [−HK], are marked with *a* or *the*, but articles are not used with nonreferential nouns,
- at Stage 2, *the* is used in [+SR] contexts and *a* in [−SR] contexts,
- at Stage 3, sensitivity to the feature [±HK] appears,
- at Stage 4, the target system of articles is used, that is, both features [±SR] and [±HK] are taken into consideration.

As far as the early stages of L2 acquisition are concerned, the most common finding that emerges from the available literature is that learners commonly overuse the definite article (Bitchener & Knoch, 2010; Chaudron & Parker, 1990; Huebner, 1983; Master, 1997; Young, 1996). This phenomenon is sometimes referred to as "*the*-flooding."

For speakers of L1s which feature articles, the findings appear to be mixed as to the sequence of *a/an* and *the* (see, e.g. Díez-Bedmar and Papp (2008) versus Thomas (1989)), while both the definite and the indefinite article seem to be mastered earlier than the zero article.

For learners with article-less L1s, studies on the acquisition of the definite article *the* and the indefinite article *a* also yield somewhat conflicting results. It seems that in the majority of studies, the definite article is used correctly earlier than the indefinite one (Master, 1997; Parrish, 1987; Sun, 2016; Thomas, 1989), but there are studies which suggest the contrary (Díez-Bedmar & Papp, 2008; Liu & Gleason, 2002; Young, 1996). Park (1996) examined ESL learners whose L1 had articles (French, German) and others who did not (Korean and Japanese). His results showed that definite-first sequence of acquisition (definite first, then indefinite) is observed whether or not the L1 possessed an article system. Of special interest is a study by Ekiert (2004), as the participants were speakers of L1 Polish. Ekiert's results show that the first article to be used by learners was *a* (in nonreferential and first-mention contexts). Additionally, the learner's output was characterized by a very substantial overuse of the zero article, which means underuse of the overt articles. Finally, of all the contexts of article, it was the generic uses, as well as the idiomatic ones, that caused Polish learners the greatest difficulty.

Similarly to Ekiert's study, the overuse of the zero article has been observed in many other studies with learners from article-less language backgrounds (Díez-Bedmar & Papp, 2008; Master, 1997; Parrish, 1987). This underuse of articles which have an overt form persists in the case of learners from article-less languages, sometimes even at high levels of proficiency (Ekiert, 2004; Kharma, 1981; Master, 1997). Even the most advanced Japanese learners in Butler's study, remained well below target norms with respect to article use. She notes that "the finer complexities of English article usage continue to challenge learners' abilities to correctly use articles" (Butler, 2002, p. 472). In Sun's

(2016) study with 18 adult ESL learners from various language back-grounds doing a cloze test on articles, the main difference between speakers of L1s with and without articles resided in the zero arti-cle, which turned out to be the most challenging of article types. At beginner and intermediate levels, the participants with article-less L1s scored much lower for zero articles than their counterparts with arti-cles in their L1. At advanced levels, the means for zero articles were comparable across groups (62% for each language type), suggesting that the zero article still poses challenges for advanced learners, due mostly to the aspect of countability, on which more will be said in the next section.

The acquisition of articles by Polish learners of English was also investigated by Świątek (2013, 2014). Participants at three proficiency levels had to supply missing articles in sentences containing obliga-tory contexts for the use of an article (the sentences were adapted from earlier studies). The results were interpreted by the author as showing that, generally, the sequence of L2 article acquisition is mostly similar to the order in L1, as evidenced by the success rates in the supplying of the correct articles by the various groups.

A considerable amount of attention is paid in the literature to the fact that beginning learners seem to overuse the definite article in the [–HK, +SR] contexts, that is, they tend to incorrectly associate the use of the definite article with specificity (Chaudron & Parker, 1990; Tar-one & Parrish, 1988; Thomas, 1989; Young, 1996).

In Thomas's study (1989) L2 learners overgeneralized *the* in first-mention contexts [+SR, –HK] but not in [–SR, –HK] contexts, which mirrors what happens in the case of L1 learners of English. The author concluded that both L1 and L2 learners tend to initially asso-ciate the use of the definite article with the feature [+SR].

Butler (2002) gave excellent examples illustrating the two trends mentioned in this and the previous section: the incorrect use of *the* in contexts perceived to be specific, and problems with article use based on wrong assumptions about countability. Examples of the learners' article choices are presented below along with the explanations (provided by the learners in an interview) of why they decided to use those articles (Butler, 2002, p. 459):

| "Japan has **the** old culture, stretching back in time more than 2,500 years…" | "…this is the, because this means Japanese culture, which is specific" |
| "Japan has Ø old culture, stretching back in time more than 2,500 years…" | "I did not insert anything here because I thought culture is not countable" |

The first example illustrated the overuse of *the* resulting from the overgeneralization of the rule of specificity. The other trend is the overuse of the zero article because of a misjudgement concerning countability. Butler's learners often assumed that abstract nouns are not countable.

5.5. STUDIES ON COUNTABILITY

Some fine-tuned analyses of the problems learners face with articles point to the connection between errors in article use and the countability of nouns (Butler, 2002; B. White, 2009; Yoon, 1993). Error analysis studies reveal that some article errors made by learners are actually very likely to be due to another error, namely a misspecification of the countability or the number of a noun, as the assignment of the count/non-count feature to nouns in interlanguage may differ from the target (Young, 1996). Errors regarding countability may have to do with the fact that learners at beginner levels tend to assume that nouns are either countable or not, and may try to rely on memorized lists of such nouns in making decisions on whether to use an article or not. In fact, nouns can commonly be used as either countable or not, depending on the intended meaning (see the discussion in 2.4), which limits the usefulness of memorizing noun status with respect to countability. Apparently, learners tend to treat countability as a fixed property of specific nouns, so they are less likely to be able to use nouns which are usually uncountable with a countable meaning in a given context (Yoon, 1993). Butler also comments on this tendency, stating that, at the beginning stages of language acquisition, countability is treated as a "fixed or static entity" (Butler, 2002, p. 466). In other words, there is insufficient awareness of nouns having the capacity to function both as countable as an uncountable, depending on the intended meaning.

It might seem that this is a problem restricted to beginners, but Butler (2002) provides an excellent example of this problem occurring in the language production of advanced learners. The specific type of problem which caused a large number of errors in Butler's study was the use of the indefinite article with abstract nouns denoting entities which are normally perceived as indivisible, but can sometimes be conceptually divided into different kinds, for example, *a warm environment, a cold environment*. The learners in Butler's study were unaware of this possibility when it existed, or alternately, they overgeneralized this principle and produced word combinations such as *a warm water, a cold water*.

Similar findings were obtained by White (2009). In this study, speakers of article-less L1s (mostly Korean), advanced ESL learners, filled in a forced-choice elicitation test. They were also asked to provide confidence ratings and explanations for their article choices. White's results indicate that with the definite article, the learners were mostly sensitive to the appropriate feature – definiteness – and were not influenced by noun type in their decisions. With the indefinite article, they were sensitive to both indefiniteness and noun type. However, with the zero article, the participants were the least sensitive to semantic context; rather, they seemed to be sensitive to countability and noun type. The learners' explanations revealed that often their wrong choices of articles were due to misidentifications of count status for abstract count nouns and non-count ones. Also, in some cases the learners seemed to choose articles on the basis of the nouns' count status alone, which resulted in the frequent use of the zero article for nouns which were believed (wrongly) to be uncountable. White concluded that some learners pay "disproportionate attention to countability," which leads to "insensitivity to semantic context" (2009, p. 28). Thus, a major problem for some ESL learners is that: "they consider the count status of the noun without considering definiteness in the semantic context. Once they perceive a noun to be uncountable, they resort to the choice of Ø" (B. White, 2009, p. 28). White also observes that in some studies, it is not always possible to tease apart countability and the effects of specificity and definiteness. For example, a learner's use or non-use of the definite article may be attributed by researchers to sensitivity to definiteness or the lack of it, whereas it may in fact be due to mistaken assumptions concerning countability. Because the learner has to take into consideration both countability and the context of the NP, he attends to countability first, which overrides any consideration of the semantic context.

5.6. ABSTRACTNESS

Another factor at play which has been identified by studies investigating learners' article use is abstractness, which in turn is related to countability. Apparently, more errors in article use occur with abstract nouns than with concrete nouns (Hua & Lee, 2005; Ogawa, 2008; B. White, 2009). In a study by Amuzie and Spinner (2013), the level of accuracy in article use was attributed not only to abstractness, but also to more nuanced aspects of abstractness, such as the nouns' degree of boundedness. Similarly, in a study by Hiki (1991), learners of English were particularly likely to misjudge the count status of nouns in the case of abstract nouns, and were least accurate when using articles with abstract nouns. In White's study (2009), the participants had significantly lower confidence ratings for their article choices in the case of abstract nouns.

5.7. ARTICLES AND LEARNERS' INTERIM RULES

Some light is thrown on the difficulties which learners have to confront when using articles in English by studies which investigate the learners' metalinguistic knowledge of the English article system, that is, the interim rules of the learners' interlanguage which are relied on at a given moment. For example, Butler (2002) analysed the process of "making sense" of the English article system by Japanese ESL learners at different levels of proficiency, who had to complete an article-fill-in-test and immediately afterwards participated in a structured interview. Such studies provide a valuable addition to the more common quantitative investigations of article use, by providing qualitative data that reveal very interesting facts about how learners struggle to make sense of the English article system by forming numerous ad-hoc working hypotheses, then discarding them, and forming new ones. Such studies also attest to the frustrating nature of the English article system, recording the learners' confusion, lack of confidence and hesitation. To quote just one of the learners who were interviewed in Butler's study (2002, p. 468):

> I know there are some words that take *the*, *garden*, for example. Wait, garden might not take *the*. I'm not confident about garden. But I learned that park takes *the*. To be honest with you, I don't know whether this is really true or not. But I use *the* anyway.

Another observation by Butler (2002) is that the learners tend to rely on syntactic or structural cues which are interpreted in an oversimplified way. For example, the learners assumed that a reference was specific if the noun was modified, which led to the production of errors such as "I made the terrible mistake" (first-mention). As a result of these tendencies, the indefinite article is bound to be underused.

However, the main observation that emerges from Butler's study is that learners at lower to intermediate proficiency levels generate large numbers of working hypotheses on which they try to rely to make correct article choices. It is clear that the learners can provide an explanation for a large number of their article-related choices; however, in most cases, they overgeneralize a "rule" or misapply one. The overall picture is that the system of rules for article use in English is such that it is actually almost impossible for lower-level learners to apply those rules, which means that attempts at teaching those rules may result in more confusion than profit.

5.8. TYPE OF TASK

It has been observed that different tasks yield different frequencies of article errors (Kharma, 1981; Tarone & Parrish, 1988). Production tasks, for example essays, or responses in interview tasks, have produced lower error rates than objective tasks, such as cloze tests. Tarone and Parrish (1988) investigated the use of articles by ESL learners in two different tasks – interviews and narratives – and found a number of differences. For example, referential definites were used more often in the narrative; they were also used more accurately. The authors explained this observation by means of the narrator's need to communicate effectively: in a narrative, it is important for the speaker to mark NPs in a way that makes it possible for the hearer to keep track of the story, and this is done mostly by means of clear anaphoric marking.

5.9. LEXICAL CHUNKS

Although the studies of article use overviewed in this chapter did not address the issue of the use of articles in lexical chunks, they sometimes make brief references to such uses. However, such mentions are extremely rare; usually in the context of the limitations of a given elicitation test or a given study. For example, White (2012) used a forced-choice elicitation test of articles, designed specifically to measure the learners' sensitivity to noun type, countability, and other characteristics. The test was accompanied by an explanations sheet, on which the learners explained their choices. The learners sometimes gave unexpected answers, on which the author commented:

> It is possible that participants' article decisions for individual dialogues were influenced not solely by semantic features and noun types, but also by previous exposure to lexical chunks. For example, Participant 18 wrote in explanation of Item 14 that she often heard her roommate say "I'm not in a mood."
>
> (B. White, 2012, p. 29)

In Young's study (Young, 1996), all NPs were examined, but some were not coded and thus excluded from the analysis, for a number of reasons. Interestingly, one of the reasons for the exclusions of some NPs is "the likelihood that they had been learned as chunks" (Young, 1996, p. 152). Unfortunately, no more details are provided on such NPs.

5.10. CONCLUSIONS

It appears that learners of English as a second language have to deal with the fact that there are no one-to-one form to meaning mappings in the system of English articles, they have to learn the properties of nouns related to countability and understand that those properties are context-dependent, they have to find out how to mark specific versus nonspecific reference, and they have to learn to take into account whether or not the context is shared between the speaker and the hearer. This sounds like a major challenge, but is not yet all, as learners will face a body of idiomatic uses which may not conform to these complex and intricate rules. Indeed, it comes as no surprise that articles are a major source of difficulty for learners of L2 English.

As could be seen from the above review, it has been established beyond any doubt that articles are more difficult to learn for speakers of article-less languages, than for speakers of mother tongues which feature similar independent prenominal morphemes. The bulk of research on articles in SLA has been done on semantic universals, and it has yielded mixed results as on how learners become sensitive to the features of definiteness and specificity.

It is unfortunate that research on language universals has so far failed to provide a clear picture of the use of articles by learners from various language backgrounds; the findings are sometimes inconclusive, and at times contradictory. Most importantly, however, interesting as they are, studies on language universals and the acquisition of articles have limited applicability to language instruction. Generative grammar consists of fundamental research rather than applied research, and it aims at modeling human language competence. There is usually little concern for how those hypotheses may serve pedagogical purposes. In fact, one of main tenets of generative grammar is that under normal circumstances, minimal exposure to human language is sufficient to trigger normal language development, suggesting limited effects of pedagogical intervention.

Another important fact is that the count/mass distinction and its current status in a learner's interlanguage affects the ability to correctly use articles. Interesting findings have been published concerning the fact that as learners struggle to make sense of the article system in English, they generate a number of hypotheses and interim rules which are often inadequate. The above overview has also shown that relatively little is known about the use of articles in idiomatic expressions and fixed phrases.

CHAPTER 6

Articles and ESL teaching

6.1. INTRODUCTION

Articles are usually considered unteachable. In the words of Gass and Selinker: "the English article system... appears to be virtually impermeable to instruction" (2008, p. 383). Testimonies to that effect can easily be found in the literature, such as a teacher's comment to the effect that the way his students use articles "bears little or no resemblance to established English practice; the students seem to use articles almost randomly" (Yamada & Matsuura, 1982, p. 50).

There are good theoretical grounds for articles to be difficult for learners, as was shown in Chapter 4, and much has been written about the various difficulties that learners face with articles. However, despite the acquisition of articles by ESL learners being quite a well-researched area (as could be seen in Chapter 5), relatively little has been said in terms of specific teaching recommendations. One problem is the low level of success with direct instruction, which is most likely due to the huge complexity of metalinguistic rules and the poor usability of such rules in language production. Articles are commonly believed to be best learnt from context, and therefore large amounts of exposure to English should facilitate acquisition. This does not mean, however, that learners exposed to a lot of input do not have problems with articles. In Ekiert's study (2004), learners from an EFL context were compared with those in an ESL context. While the sequence of the acquisition of articles was similar, the EFL learners were more accurate in their article choices. This appears to contradict the belief that exposure to natural language is the best way to learn the "unteachable" articles. However, due to small group size and differences in learner profiles, those conclusions are only tentative.

6.2. ARTICLES AND THE EFFICACY OF CORRECTIVE FEEDBACK

The bulk of research on the teaching of articles comes from studies on the efficacy of corrective feedback, as articles are often selected as the target language feature in such studies. Corrective feedback is defined as the information provided to L2 learners about the ill-formedness of their production (Stefanou & Révész, 2015). In the studies which involve articles, the corrective feedback tends to be written. Corrective feedback is usually classified as either indirect (when only an indication that an error has been made is provided) or direct (when the correct form is provided as well). Additionally, corrective feedback may be accompanied by metalinguistic explanations, that is, the rules behind the use of the selected language feature.

Very interesting pedagogical considerations arise from a study by Sheen (2007a). The aim of that study was to compare the effects of different types of corrective feedback on the learning of articles, and to see if the effects would be mediated by learner aptitude and attitude. One type of treatment involved the provision of feedback in the form of teacher's recasts of the learners' article errors, while the other type was metalinguistic explanation (accompanied by the corrected form). Sheen found that the latter type of feedback was clearly far superior to the former: learners who received the "metalinguistic" feedback showed gains on both the immediate post-test and the delayed post-test, whereas the learners who received feedback in the form of recasts performed on the same level as the control group.

In another, similar study by the same author (Sheen, 2007b), the two types of feedback were investigated when used in dealing with errors in texts written by learners of mixed L1 backgrounds (including Polish). The target feature was article use for first mention and anaphoric reference. As in the case of the oral task study, direct corrective feedback which incorporated metalinguistic explanations and provided the correct form proved to be the superior form of feedback, resulting in significant gains both immediately after treatment and on a delayed post-test. However, while the recasts used in the oral task study did not lead to any gains, in the study of written feedback, corrective feedback without metalinguistic explanations produced some positive results. They were inferior to the metalinguistic explanations feedback, but still superior to the control group. The study thus shows that the learners clearly benefited more from the provision of feedback than when given no feedback. Also, the superiority of metalinguistic explanations was mostly observed on the delayed post-test. This finding is explained by the author by referring to the distinction between two levels of awareness: noticing and understanding. While noticing involves giving attention to specific language forms, understanding involves the awareness of the rule that underlies the choice of those language forms. While understanding entails noticing, the reverse is not necessarily true. Noticing is a crucial step towards acquisition, but understanding leads to greater and deeper learning, and facilitates future learning, hence the gains on the delayed post-test.

Another interesting study investigating direct corrective feedback and metalinguistic explanation was carried out by Shintani and Ellis (2013). The authors found that only the latter type of feedback had any effect on the learner's use of the English indefinite article. They examined the learners' indefinite article use in a free writing task (which, they argue, is more likely to reflect implicit knowledge) and an error correction task (presented as a measurement of explicit knowledge). Direct corrective feedback had no impact on the learners' use of articles: learners who had their articles corrected did not improve as a result. On the contrary, learners who had the rules behind article use explained to them benefited from the treatment insofar as the error correction task after treatment and the first texts they wrote after treatment showed improvement; however, in subsequent writing tasks this effect wore off. Shintani and Ellis interpret this finding as meaning that neither type of treatment benefited implicit knowledge, because one did not yield any results, and the other only registered briefly, so it only temporarily affected explicit knowledge.

Another study by the same authors (Shintani, Ellis, & Suzuki, 2014) yielded even more pessimistic results as far as the teaching of articles is concerned. In that study, adult pre-intermediate Japanese learners were provided with direct corrective feedback and metalinguistic explanations with respect to two target features: the indefinite article (for first-mention contexts) and the hypothetical conditional. Interestingly, the study led to gains in the use of the hypothetical conditional, but not to an improved command of the indefinite article. In other words, in that study, the (relatively complex) grammatical structure of the hypothetical conditional proved to be more "teachable" than the use of the indefinite article. The authors explain this by saying that the learners are more likely to attend to features that contribute more to the global meaning of texts.

The effectiveness of feedback with respect to articles was also investigated in a study with Polish participants. Zabor and Rychlewska

(2015) looked at written error correction and found that all types of corrective feedback under investigation were superior to the results obtained for the control group, which confirmed that corrective feedback does bring some improvements to the learners' use of articles. What is particularly interesting in their study is that the feedback was useful especially when it included metalinguistic information and when it was combined with the inductive type of formal instruction.

However, there are also studies which show that corrective feedback results in improvement in article use, but the inclusion of metalinguistic knowledge does not make a difference. Research involving advanced learners (Bitchener & Knoch, 2010) confirmed that even at an advanced level, learners can make further improvement in their use of articles as the result of corrective feedback, with or without metalinguistic explanation. In this study, it was again the use of indefinite articles with first mention nouns that was the subject of investigation. A study that looked at the use of articles for specific and generic plural reference (Stefanou & Révész, 2015) also found that the provision of feedback is superior to providing no feedback, but the inclusion of metalinguistic information does not make a difference.

Summing up, existing studies on the efficacy of corrective feedback bring mixed results. In some studies (Shintani et al., 2014) feedback did not result in improvement, or resulted only in temporary gains (Shintani & Ellis, 2013). In other studies, feedback resulted in improved article use (Bitchener & Knoch, 2010; Sheen, 2007b, 2007a; Stefanou & Révész, 2015; Zabor & Rychlewska, 2015) but the results were mixed with respect to the inclusion of metalinguistic explanations, which were found to enhance learning only in some of these studies.

Even though the findings are mixed, they seem to give a general picture of the superiority of written corrective feedback over no feedback, and of direct over indirect feedback. This seems to contradict the remarks made earlier in this book about the seemingly unteachable nature of the English article system. If articles are as resistant to teaching as common wisdom holds, one would expect their use not to improve much as the result of corrective feedback, and one would expect metalinguistic explanations to be of little use, given the high level of complexity of the rules needed to explain article use. This apparent contradiction warrants an explanation.

It should be noted that the above studies investigated article use, but they selected the specific types of article use which are the easiest ones to teach, that is, ones involving a correspondence between the language pattern and the metalinguistic proposition (to use the terminology introduced in Chapter 4). For example, Sheen's results (2007a, 2007b) leave no doubt that learners benefited from corrective feedback, especially with metalinguistic explanations, but it should be noted that only two specific uses of articles were investigated: the indefinite article for first-mention referents, and the definite article for anaphoric mention, with the two presented in combination. This is the kind of article use which is often selected for research studies, of the type "I saw a man. The man was tall." This particular use of the indefinite and definite article, especially in combination, is easy to explain. Potentially endless new combinations of words can be generated using this principle, which makes this pattern more teachable than other uses of articles. In fact, this particular use of articles may be the most unproblematic of all.

Because of this consideration, the studies on corrective feedback cannot provide conclusive information on the teachability of articles. This is partly because such studies are not designed to investigate the learning of English articles as such. Their main aim tends to be investigating what types of corrective feedback lead to learning gains, and articles are chosen simply as a convenient sample target language feature, with only a specific type of article use selected for investigation (for example, the use of the indefinite article in first-mention contexts). To find out to what extent the use of articles actually improves as the result of corrective feedback, and to what extent their use improves after treatment with metalinguistic information, we need a study which would measure the improvement over time in the learners' use of articles in all types of contexts, not just in the more "rule-based" contexts such as first-mention nouns.

6.3. OTHER TREATMENTS AND RECOMMENDATIONS CONCERNING THE TEACHING OF ARTICLES

Apart from studies which investigate the efficacy of corrective feedback, there are some other accounts of successful pedagogical interventions in the area of articles. Miller (2005) describes an improvement in her ESL learners at an American university, after a pedagogical treatment which involved discovery techniques combined with an explanation regarding the role of countability and definiteness.

Gillian (2017) designed an e-learning tool for the practice of English articles, specifically designed to help Polish learners aged 11–14, which has been shown to give superior teaching results compared to traditional instruction. This is a very innovative approach in that it utilizes the potential of an e-learning platform to practice articles specifically, and it adopts a "game based learning" approach – defined by the author as "a learning approach where learning and interactive entertainment are combined to create a fun and engaging experience for students in learning contexts designed by teachers" (Gillian, 2017, p. 82). At the same time, the tool is traditional in the sense that it is organized around the typical pedagogical rules that are usually used for the teaching of articles.

Some other publications make specific recommendations concerning the teaching of articles, though this is generally rare. White (2009) recommends that article instruction should involve determination of definiteness before determination of count status. Because (misguided)

consideration of countability often interferes with learners' consideration of the semantic context of a NP, White argues that:

> [L]earners should be encouraged to contemplate definiteness before
> countability. A definite context (with common nouns) will yield the
> definite article irrespective of the count status of the NP. Thus, teach-
> ers might guide their students to consider countability only after
> indefinite contexts have been determined. To help learners more
> effectively determine the definiteness or indefiniteness of a NP, teach-
> ers may want to emphasize the discourse context, especially the per-
> spectives of the interlocutors (i.e., the speaker and the hearer). Learn-
> ers can be guided to consider the speaker's presumptions about the
> hearer's knowledge.
>
> (B. White, 2009, p. 28)

White also recommends that learners should be trained to consider discourse context to determine definiteness, and finally, that
they should be made aware of the need for a flexible approach to noun
countability, by considering the different conceptualizations of countability. White recommends drawing on the work of Wierzbicka (1988)
and the concept of individuation as presented by Yule (1998). A zero
article before a noun means that its referent lacks clear boundaries
and thus resists individuation. An indefinite article before a noun
suggests that its referent possesses boundaries and can be construed
as an individual entity. Appropriate activities would involve making
the learners consider the same noun across different contexts.

The majority of Polish scholars who have devoted attention to the
teaching and learning of articles seem to share the belief in the potential of explicit instruction (Gozdawa-Gołębiowski, 2003; Paradowski,
2006, 2008; Scheffler, 2007). Such instruction should focus on making
the learners aware of crosslinguistic differences and similarities with
respect to the structural properties of language.

Paradowski recommends the "language interface" method introduced by Gozdawa-Gołębiowski (2003), in which the teaching of new
L2 structures is preceded by awareness-raising explications concerning the working of equivalent or comparable mechanisms in the L1. As
Paradowski explains,

> language-awareness tasks sensitize the learner to language phenom-
> ena which are present in both his/her L1 and the TL [target language],
> but whose overt realization in the two languages may differ. Learners
> discover whether the L1 rules are operative in the L2 and vice versa.
> The teacher's task is to demonstrate to the learners through compar-
> ative analysis that they already know something which they have so
> far regarded as mysterious. This eases the burden and is greatly facil-
> itative in lowering the affective filter.
>
> (Paradowski, 2008, pp. 232–233)

Moreover, the new structures or forms may be practiced first in the L1,
and only then in the L2. In the case of articles, the relevant L1 feature
would be the sequencing of information in Polish sentences.

In a similar vein, Scheffler (2007) recommends translation activities as a way of sensitizing learners to contrastive aspects. In his opinion, translation activities are useful, because they enable the teacher to
point out to the students that some of the meanings conveyed by the
English articles are rendered in Polish by other means, for example
by means of the sequence of elements in a sentence. To illustrate this,
Scheffler (2007, pp. 61–62) quotes examples given by Szwedek (1976,
p. 57). In the following two sets of sentences, only the first one can be
understood as pertaining to one and the same woman:

Widziałem w oknie kobietę. Po chwili kobieta wyszła z domu.
[I saw a woman in the window. After a moment, the woman came
out of the house.]

Widziałem w oknie kobietę. Po chwili z domu wyszła kobieta.
[I saw a woman in the window. After a moment, a woman came out
of the house.]

Presenting such sentences to learners of English should make it possible for them to realize that they are already familiar with the concepts
of new versus given information. Unfortunately, not all uses and meanings of the English articles (not even a majority) yield themselves to this
type of instruction. Actually, it is mostly the indefiniteness of first-mention nouns that compares neatly with the information flow structure in
Polish. Other features of Polish which share some meanings and uses
with the English articles, such as the Polish definite (demonstrative) and
indefinite pronouns (*ten, ta, to, jakiś, jakaś, jakieś*, etc.), as well as the
numeral *jeden* („one"), can be only presented as equivalents of the articles in certain specific cases, and could result in confusion if the learners tried to rely on the assumed equivalence in a systematic manner.
A critical view of the idea to use contrastive data to teach the English
articles to Polish learners has been expressed by Król-Markefka (2008),
who conducted an exploratory empirical study which showed that Polish learners of English are not very sensitive to the feature of definiteness as encoded in the word order in their L1. The author concluded that:

> ... tracing the ways in which [definiteness] may be encoded in both
> languages would place a double cognitive burden on the learner's
> mental processing. ... making students aware of the devices which
> they automatically use to express (in)definiteness in Polish is likely
> to introduce unnecessary complications and, consequently, hinder
> rather than facilitate language acquisition.
>
> (Król-Markefka, 2008, p. 111)

An important trend in the teaching of articles comes from cognitive linguistics. This field of linguistics has generally been a source

of inspiration for language teaching for some time now (see Bielak, 2011; Holme, 2007; Littlemore, 2001; Tyler, 2012).

The work of Epstein (see section 3.3) was applied in a study conducted by Hinenoya and Lyster (2015) with Japanese ESL learners. They compared the efficacy of two different instructional treatments, both computer-assisted, devoted to teaching the definite article. While one treatment focussed on the concept of identifiability, the other was based on the concept of mental spaces (MS), employing the notion of accessibility as formulated by Epstein (2002).

The authors analysed a large number of randomly extracted instances of definite article use, and grouped the non-generic uses into four types: (1) structural use, i.e., direct structural anaphoras (e.g. *A ball was on the table. The ball suddenly rolled and fell off*); (2) the "visible in the situation" usage (e.g. *Here is the bathroom*); (3) the "visible in the mind" category (e.g. *Where is the bathroom?*); 4) the inclusive/associative usage (e.g. *I've just been to a wedding. The bride wore blue*). While in the case of the first two types, the explanations offered by traditional accounts and the ones put forwards by cognitive linguists almost entirely coincide, the other two types can profit from a cognitive interpretation, in which accessibility is operationalized as the activation of schemata. A schema is "a body of knowledge that is acquired through experiences in life and is stored (to be accessed) in our mental dictionary" (Hinenoya & Lyster, 2015, p. 400). In 3), it is unlikely that the speaker has a specific bathroom in mind, as the location of the bathroom is unknown to him/her, and it is even possible that there may be no bathroom or that there may be more than one. In such cases, according to Hinenoya and Lyster, traditional accounts of definite article use are not very successful, whereas the MS approach can be used to activate the appropriate mental space, in this case, the schema of a house, which typically includes a bathroom. In 4), the mention of a wedding activates the schema of a wedding, which involves the presence of a bride.

The findings of the study confirmed the hypothesis that the MS approach is particularly helpful with types 3) and 4) of article use when it comes to Japanese learners. The authors see the pedagogical potential of the concept of accessibility, and they say that, "despite the absence of linguistic equivalents in their first language, (…) such learners are nonetheless equipped with a cognitive capacity for interpreting article usages through mental space configurations" (Hinenoya & Lyster, 2015, p. 400).

Attempts to apply concepts taken from cognitive linguistics to the teaching of articles to speakers of L1 Polish have been made by Król-Markefka (Król-Markefka, 2010; Król, 2005), who found them promising. Król-Markefka argues that cognitive-based approaches make it possible to provide students with general, conceptually-motivated rules for the use of articles.

It seems that the pedagogy of articles has not been affected much by the recent trends which emphasise the role of phraseology in language learning (more on this topic will be said in the following chapter). Only recently, a study by Shin and Kim (2017) explored the connection between formulaic sequences (more specifically, lexical bundles, which will be discussed in the next chapter) and the acquisition of articles by learners of L2 English at different proficiency levels. In view of the shortcomings of pedagogical rules on article use, and the high level of difficulty that articles present to learners, the authors decided to investigate whether lexical bundles can help L2 learners to improve their article use. The pedagogical tool they developed resulted in significant improvement in article use for learners of various language backgrounds and proficiency levels.

6.4. THE TREATMENT OF ARTICLES IN TEACHING MATERIALS AND PEDAGOGICAL GRAMMARS

The way English articles are presented, explained and practiced shows some similarity across the wide range of textbooks currently available. Despite numerous differences, articles in pedagogical materials are presented as essentially rule-governed, in keeping with the well-established status of articles as a "grammatical" topic (Holmes, 1988; Hsu, 2008). Exercises on articles are always found in the "grammar" sections of textbooks. The main rules (differently named in various textbooks) revolve around countability, definiteness and specificity (Ekiert, 2007). For example, *the* is introduced as indicating common ground / shared knowledge / referents identifiable to both interlocutors, *etc.* The textbooks usually contain the most basic rules about the indefinite article, concerning the impossibility to use it with a plural (**a tables*) and with non-count nouns (**a water*). Another frequent rule found in textbooks concerns direct anaphora: the indefinite article subsequently becomes definite upon the second mention (e.g. *I saw a player leaving the game. The player was hurt.*). Textbooks also usually provide an explanation for the use of the zero article, i.e. the possible omission of articles for generic meanings, as in the sentence *English parsley has curly leaves* (Parrott, 2000, p. 46).

Because of the challenging character of the main rules for article use, most textbooks resort to a set of practical rules, often called "rules of thumb" (Parrott, 2000, p. 48). These rules of thumb seek to account for a certain number of exceptions to basic rules by grouping those exceptions and showing that they follow the same pattern. A frequent rule of thumb aims at accounting for the fact that the article is dropped before some nouns that denote institutions (e.g. *school, church, prison, hospital*). Although countable, they will be used without a definite article, provided the primary function of those places is being referred to.

In addition, most pedagogical grammars and textbooks make a connection between article use and idiomaticity, by acknowledging that there are some "fixed" or "idiomatic" expressions in which articles are used differently than the available rules would suggest (for example, *living hand to mouth, all of a sudden, in front* vs. *in the back*, or *game of cat and mouse*). This strengthens the impression that the unpredictable use of articles is limited to a handful of idiomatic expressions, which constitute exceptions to an otherwise rule-governed system.

It has been pointed out that the importance assigned to those rules is often out of touch with descriptive accounts of English grammar and corpus findings. Generally, the pedagogical treatment does not correspond well to what corpus analyses reveal about article use (Yoo, 2009). For example, textbooks tend to overemphasize direct anaphoric use of the definite article compared to the actual frequency of this type of article in corpora (Yoo, 2009). As Hinenoya and Lyster point out, the usage of the definite article which they call "inclusive/associative" (of the type "I've just been to a wedding. The bride wore blue," i.e., indirectly anaphorical,) is very frequently used in reality, whereas it is rarely presented in textbooks (Hinenoya & Lyster, 2015).

An analysis of nine commonly used grammar textbooks with exercises with respect to articles was conducted by Król-Markefka (2012), who pointed out considerable differences in how the usage of articles is presented, and noted a significant amount of confusion and lack of clarity. According to the author, the rules presented in the analysed textbooks are inadequate especially in terms of their predictivity and discriminatory power. The main shortcomings of the textbook rules are: "1) lack of consistency, which is confusing and hinders meaningful learning; 2) numerous 'uses' and exceptions, which makes the rules less memorable; 3) lack of unity and meaningful justifications, which makes the rules and their functions not so easy to understand; in consequence, the learners cannot make their own contextually-dependent decisions when using articles" (Król-Markefka, 2012, p. 105).

It seems that the large number of rules presented in textbooks, along with their lack of predictivity, is the main source of difficulty in applying those rules. A learner, faced with the need to communicate a specific message, can easily think of a number of rules, sometimes contradictory ones, that all seem to apply. I have explained this in an earlier publication:

> The entire point of having rules is that they are generalizable, that is, productive. A learner of English, knowing the rule for the third person singular ending of verbs, being familiar with sentences such as *Alice likes flowers*, or *Chris loves fast cars*, and knowing the verb *hate* can come up with a correct sentence such as *Alice hates Chris* by means of applying that rule. With articles, a similar action is much more difficult, if not entirely impossible, because very often all of the rules seem to apply. For example, a learner may say "I need to go to a bathroom," because there are several bathrooms in the house he happens to be in, bathrooms are clearly countable, and he does not need to use a specific one. He may equally well think it is acceptable to say, "I need to go to bathroom," because he intends to make use of the primary function of the bathroom.
>
> (Leśniewska, 2017, p. 68)

6.5. CONCLUSIONS

As this chapter has shown, accounts of successful pedagogical interventions with respect to articles are not numerous, but they do exist.
The teaching of articles has been studied mostly within the framework of studies on the efficacy of corrective feedback. While these
studies tend to show the superiority of feedback over no feedback,
and they usually report better results when metalinguistic explanations are provided, it has to be remembered that such studies focus
on selected types of article use (most commonly, the use of the indefinite article for first mention, or the definite article for anaphoric use),
that is, the type of uses of articles which is are relatively easy to iso-
late and straightforward to teach by means of rule explanation. This
leads to the tentative conclusion that, among all types of article uses,
there are some that may be very resistant to teaching, and are more
likely to be produced correctly mostly through collocational competence, and some that are graspable for learners at the level of a general "grammar" rule.

Studies on the efficacy of corrective feedback also tell us, indirectly, something interesting about the reason for the problematic
character of articles in ESL acquisition. They show that simple recasts
or corrections (without metalinguistic explanations) bring negligible,
if any, improvement in the learners' performance (as in, most notably,
Sheen, 2007a). In Sheen's study, this lack of improvement occurred
even though the recasts were focused solely on articles. Even more
striking is the fact that the learners did not even notice that articles
were the focus of the recasts, as evidenced by a questionnaire incorporated in the study. This persistent failure to notice article-related
corrections strongly suggests that one of the reasons for their seem-
ing "unteachability" may be that they are largely ignored by learners,
as they are not perceived as salient.

Among the innovative approaches to the teaching of articles are explorations of the pedagogical potential of concepts taken from cognitive linguistics, as well as methods based on the application of contrastive studies to the teaching of articles. However, opinions on the usefulness of those approaches are mixed, and empirical evidence remains scarce.

CHAPTER 7

Formulaicity

7.1. INTRODUCTION

In our understanding of how language works, the word is a crucial element. The lexicon is usually seen as collection of individual words, which form the building blocks of larger utterances. One important characteristic of words is that they seem to participate in different kinds of "lexical partnerships" (Singleton, 2000, p. 47). Because some words are often found in the company of certain other words, lexical partnerships of various kinds have long been recognized in language research.

As the ubiquity of such language phenomena is increasingly noticed, the term "formulaicity" seems to be emerging as the most popular "umbrella" term used to refer to the quality of language that makes it impossible to reduce it simply to individual words and syntactic rules, and to refer to the many different kinds of connections between words in a language (e.g. Meunier, 2012).[17]

---

[17] Obviously, having a term with that general a meaning renders it useless for any kind of precise denotation of any specific phenomenon. In fact, it has been

To provide the broadest possible definition of formulaicity, it is useful to take as the starting point the traditional "slot and filler" approach to language. In this view, for each "slot" along the syntagmatic axis, one word is chosen from a number of options available along the paradigmatic axis, depending on the intended meaning. The choices for each slot, however, are restricted to certain classes of words by syntagmatic restraints which result from the syntactic rules of the language. In its broadest sense, formulaicity can be taken to mean all the phenomena which affect how words are combined together which fall outside the "slot and filler" model. Boers and Lindstromberg offer a good practical definition of formulaicity: "the use of word strings that have become conventionalized in a given language as attested by native-speaker judgment and/or corpus data" (2012, p. 83). Many authors use definitions of formulaic expressions which are based on the assumed holistic processing, such as: "frequent multiword combinations that are stored and retrieved holistically from the mental lexicon at the moment of speech" (Nekrasova, 2009, p. 647). However, such definitions are better avoided, since proving that multiword combinations are stored/retrieved holistically is in itself problematic, as will be explained in more detail below.

---

argued that using formulaicity as an umbrella term brings more confusion than good, as it creates the impression that different researchers are discussing the same phenomenon, whereas they are in fact talking about very different constructs (see Myles & Cordier, 2016). However, once the term has been appropriated by researchers working with very different theoretical frameworks and methodologies, there is no going back. It would be nothing short of a miracle if a consensus was achieved across academia as to which narrow sense the term "formulaic" should be reserved for. In this situation, it makes sense to use it as a much-needed hold-all term. The term will also be used in this study in its most general meaning. Another popular umbrella term is *phraseology*, usually defined as an area of academic inquiry which deals with the formulaic nature of language (see eg. Granger & Meunier, 2008).

It is usually assumed that the rationale for the existence of formulaicity in language has to do with advantages it offers in terms of ease
and speed of processing, as "formulaic sequences have been argued
to minimize encoding work for both the speaker and addressee, thus
allowing for the construction of fluent spoken discourse" (Nekrasova,
2009, p. 647). In the words of Conklin and Schmitt (2012, p. 45):

> It makes sense that our brains would make use of a relatively abun-
> dant resource (long-term memory) to compensate for a relative lack
> in another (working memory) by storing frequently occurring for-
> mulaic sequences. These could then be easily retrieved and used
> without the need to compose them online through word selection
> and grammatical sequencing.

The implications of this widely accepted assumption, as well as empirical research supporting it, will be presented and discussed later in
this chapter.

Myles and Cordier (2016) argue that studies on formulaicity suffer from the confusion between what they call "speaker-external"
and "speaker-internal" discussions of formulaicity, which should
be clearly distinguished. Speaker-external formulaicity can be
observed in language. For example, formulaic sequences may be
defined on the basis of their frequency of occurrence in a corpus.
When claims are made about the psycholinguistic reality of formulaic language, the approach is speaker-internal. In the overview
below, I first look at what could be called by Myles and Cordier
the speaker-external approaches to formulaic language, and then
move on to the speaker-internal ones, before discussing the aspect
which is of crucial importance to this study, namely the connection
between the two.

7.2. SPEAKER-EXTERNAL FORMULAICITY

As has been said above, words enter into various lexical partnerships with one another. However, the lack of a universally accepted taxonomy, as well as the fact that interest in word combinations comes from many different theoretical perspectives, result in a substantial amount of confusion. Among the most frequently discussed phenomena related to the lexical partnerships of words are "idioms," "collocations," "restricted collocations," "collostructions," "binomials," "formulas," "chunks," "prefabs," "routines," "lexical phrases," "fixed phrases," "lexical bundles" and "n-grams." Except for the last two, these terms are sometimes used with different meanings by different authors, and their meaning is not always rigorously defined. All of these concepts are related to the fact that certain words co-occur, but there are important differences among them. Perhaps the best-studied one of the above categories, idioms, are often opaque in meaning and are non-compositional. For example, the meaning of the expression *on/over the grapevine* cannot be deduced from its component parts. However, this quality is far from being a defining feature of idioms, as their meaning may be deducible, as in the case of, for example, the expression *a drop in the ocean*. To further complicate the situation, the distinctions involved in classifying such expressions are not binary. One could argue, for instance, that there are degrees of opacity, and the phrase *a fair-weather friend* is more comprehensible than *a different kettle of fish*.

The term "multi-word units" (MWUs) seems to be emerging as the most universally accepted general name for idioms, collocations, binomials, phrasal verbs, *etc.* (e.g. Wolter & Yamashita, 2018). This usage will be followed here, even though it should be noted that the term is misleading, as the name "unit" overemphasises the holistic nature of such expressions, which is debatable in view of the fact that most MWUs can be decomposed into parts, and that the co-occurrence of words is a matter of degrees.

The wide range of terminology used to refer to MWUs reflects the fact that interest in lexical co-occurrence comes from various disciplines: linguistics, lexicography, corpus linguistics, language processing, discourse analysis, second language acquisition research, and second language pedagogy. The terms "collocation," "lexical bundles," "*n*-grams," *etc.* are used in corpus linguistics in reference to the fact that words co-occur in corpora. "Prefabricated units," "prefabs" and "chunks" are discussed in studies of language acquisition and processing to indicate that certain word combinations are acquired and/or processed as wholes; "formulas" or "formulaic language" are terms which emphasize the fact that many phrases can be used repeatedly in certain contexts instead of having to be generated anew each time; the terms "institutionalized phrases," "fixed expressions" and "routines" suggest that many phrases can be used to achieve particular functions in predictable social situations – the emphasis here is on the conventionality of language.

What is important to note is that the various types of MWUs may display very different properties. They may be defined on the basis of intuitive criteria, corpus data, or pragmatic function, or any combination of those. They may range in opacity from opaque to transparent, in frequency from very frequent to relatively rare (as is the case with some idioms), and in the degree of fixedness, from completely "frozen" phrases to ones which allow for a certain degree of manipulation.

A very important concept in the study of formulaic language is that of collocation. The term does not have a single, widely accepted definition,[18] but – generally speaking – it refers to the habitual co-oc-

---

[18] In keeping with the origin of the word *collocation*, i.e. the "placing together" of words (from the Latin *collocare*: *co* (together) + *locare* (to place)). In this sense the term has been used since the mid-20th century, when it was popularized by

currence of words (Cruse, 1986, p. 40). Collocations are often defined as words that co-occur more frequently than their respective frequencies would predict (e.g. Jones & Sinclair, 1974). For that reason, a word "predicts" the word(s) which typically follow(s). Laufer and Waldman (2011, pp. 648–649) provide a definition of collocations which corresponds very well to what seems to be the most common understanding of the term in contemporary literature:

> We regard collocations as habitually occurring lexical combinations that are characterized by restricted co-occurrence of elements and relative transparency of meaning. Restricted co-occurrence distinguishes collocations from free combinations in which the individual words are easily replaceable following the rules of grammar. Relative semantic transparency of collocations, on the other hand, distinguishes them from idioms whose meaning is much less transparent than that of collocations and is very often opaque because it cannot be understood from the words that compose them.

This is also the understanding of "collocation" which is of most relevance to second language acquisition and language teaching contexts, as, from a language acquisition perspective, the most important feature of collocations is their lack of predictability from a "words-and-rules" point of view. Apart from knowing the meaning of *do* and *homework*, a L2 learner of English must also know that *homework* collocates with *do* and not with *make*. This is why collocations are challenging for learners in production, and not so much in comprehension.

Firth and his followers. However, there is a wide array of definitions of the term which are completely different. Firth originally used the term in a broader sense, referring to all kinds of co-occurrences at various levels of language, for example to alliteration. Nation uses the term "collocation" to describe "any generally accepted grouping of words into phrases or clauses" (Nation, 2001, p. 317).

Collocations can be variously defined and classified with reference to frequency of co-occurrence, restrictions on commutability, semantic characteristics, the notion of familiarity (the fact that certain phrases are recognized by native speakers as familiar), or habitual use. Because of the availability of large corpora and the ease with which frequency information can be extracted from them, a very common approach to collocation is a frequency-based one, where collocations are identified on the basis of automated searches only. By researching recurrent combinations of words in corpora, it is possible to easily obtain information on which words typically collocate, either side-by-side or within a certain span of words. A basic measure of how common a collocation is in a language is its frequency in the corpus. However, one can also measure the exclusivity of co-occurrence, that is,

> the extent to which the two words appear solely or predominantly in each other's company, usually expressed in terms of the relationship between the number of times when they are seen together as opposed to the number of times when they are seen separately in the corpus.
> (Gablasova, Brezina, & McEnery, 2017, p. 160)

This measure is known as the Mutual Information [MI] score. For example, *torrential* is very often found with *rain*, *glaringly* with *obvious*.

Another important term – this used only in corpus-based studies – is *lexical bundle*. Introduced by Biber and colleagues (Biber, 2009; Biber et al., 1999; Conrad & Biber, 2004), the term denotes the most frequently recurring sequences of words in a collection of texts. Because bundles are identified using corpus analysis software, which automatically retrieves word sequences which occur most frequently, they do not necessarily coincide with multiword units defined according to other criteria, for example pragmatic or discursive ones, nor do they tend to be complete structural units (see e.g. Conrad & Biber,

2004). For example, they may incorporate clausal boundaries, as in the bundle *I know that I*, or they may contain incomplete nominal chunks, for example, *as the result of*. Lexical bundles are also known as "*n*-grams," with *n* standing for the number of words in the bundle. The lexical bundle (*n*-gram) approach identifies strings of adjacent words of a given length. In contrast, collocations can be found in the corpus with a predetermined degree of proximity, as specified by the window span set for a specific search.

To what extent is language formulaic? Conklin and Schmitt (2012) discuss seven studies which used very different methods to answer this question. For example, researchers count the percentage of identical strings in stretches of talk, or they look at the percentage of text that is made up of lexical bundles. Of course, the exact amount of formulaic language will inevitably depend on the method used to identify formulaic elements. However, the average from this group of studies gives a certain rough idea, and Conklin and Schmitt (2012) conclude that between one third and one half of discourse is formulaic in nature.

7.3. SPEAKER-INTERNAL FORMULAICITY

7.3.1. THE IDIOM PRINCIPLE

Studies on large corpora of texts have proven beyond doubt that certain word combinations tend to reoccur, but as such they tell us nothing about the reasons why this happens. It is commonly assumed that this tendency is a reflection of a psycholinguistic phenomenon which makes it easier for humans to retrieve and process familiar combinations of words, and that is why they use them more frequently. Already in the 1980s, in a much-cited paper, Pawley and Syder sought to explain what these authors saw as "two puzzles for linguistic theory." The two puzzles were two intriguing characteristics of the speech of native language users, namely "native-like selection" and "native-like fluency." The first one denotes the ability to produce phrases which are the natural form of expression, rather than "odd" collocations. The other characteristic – "fluency"– was described as puzzling because "human capacities for encoding novel speech in advance or while speaking appear to be severely limited, yet speakers commonly produce fluent multi-clause utterances which exceed these limits" (Pawley & Syder, 1983, p. 191). Comparing recordings of spontaneous speech, Pawley and Syder observed that some expressions – e.g. *I don't need anyone to tell me what to do* – were relatively pause-free and delivered faster than the normal rate for language production. The authors argued that both native-like selection and fluency provide the evidence for the fact that "fluent and idiomatic control of a language rests to a considerable extent on knowledge of a body of 'sentence stems' which are 'institutionalized' or 'lexicalized'" (Pawley & Syder, 1983, p. 191). The fact that chunks can be recalled from memory does not mean that they are not analysable into segments. The speakers can always use their ability to construct an infinite number of new sentences on the basis of a finite set of grammatical rules as one of the modes which is available to them, but they "do not exercise the creative potential of syntactic rules to anything like their full extent, and that, indeed, if they did so they would not be accepted as exhibiting native-like control of the language" (1983, p. 193).

It should be noted here that Pawley and Syder actually combined two elements in their model: a pragmatic one and a psycholinguistic one. "Lexicalised sentence stems" play a particular pragmatic role, they have a specialized function in discourse, and this is connected to their pragmatic non-compositionality. In the words of Weinert, "certain language sequences have conventionalized meanings which are used in certain predictable situations" (Weinert, 1995, p. 196). That meaning may not be clear from the literal meaning of the expression.

Many of the examples given by Pawley and Syder refer to the kind of language choices which one would normally call "choosing the right expression for the right situation." The other aspect is psycholinguistic, as they claim that "memorized sentences" and "lexicalised sentence stems" are to some extent processed as wholes, as ready-made chunks of language.

Another linguist who is often credited with bringing the concept of those two modes of processing into linguistics is John Sinclair. Because of his ground-breaking research on large samples of language, Sinclair is brought the study of long authentic texts into the centre of attention in linguistics (Stubbs, 2009). His well-known distinction between the "open-choice principle" and the "idiom principle" was based on the idea of dual, simultaneous access to two modes of processing. On the one hand, any speaker can use language in the "open-choice" mode, that is, in the "slot and filler" system mentioned above, with a number of syntagmatic choices available for each slot along the paradigm, with the only restriction being imposed by syntactic rules. On the other hand, the speaker also has access to "a large number of semi-preconstructed phrases that constitute single choices, even though they might appear to be analysable into segments" (Sinclair, 1991, p. 110), which makes it possible to produce language according to the "idiom principle." Both of those modes are at the disposal of any speaker, and they are not necessarily exclusive; to the contrary, it seems more likely that they are used at the same time, in different proportions. Sinclair thus changed the emphasis in linguistics from the previously overestimated role of paradigmatic choice to syntagmatic constraints in linear sequences (Stubbs, 2009).

A similar distinction was made by Skehan (1998), who wrote about two modes of processing available to language users. One operates on the level of grammatical rules, which make it possible to generate novel utterances by putting individual words together, for example when precision of expression or creativity is needed. The second mode is based on memorized multi-word items, which can be quickly retrieved, enabling fluency.

It should be noted that the above approaches propose a certain duality: there are two modes of processing, they can be used interchangeably, and they complement each other. It stands to reason that both modes of processing co-exist, and speakers have access to both individual items and entire chunks. One could at this point ask the same question which was asked at the end of the previous section with respect to language processing: to what extent is language formulaic? If the two modes co-exist, are they used to the same extent? The "dual" models seem to imply a fifty-fifty share. However, some scholars strongly emphasize the role of the formulaic mode of processing, as if giving it priority. According to Wray (Wray, 2002a, 2002b), "formulaic processing is the default," and "construction out of, and reduction into, smaller units by rule occurs only as necessary" (Wray, 2002b, p. 119). According to Wray, evidence for this formulaic nature of language storage and processing can be found in the multiple irregularities of all kinds which are so commonly observed in all natural languages:

> if we only create and understand utterances by applying rules to words and morphemes, it is difficult to see why irregularity should be tolerated, let alone why an item or construction should progress from regular, to marked, to antiquated, to a fossilized historical relic.
>
> (Wray, 2002b, p. 118)

Indeed, the existence of such irregularities is bound to be connected with the formulaic character of language; however, they do not prove that formulaic processing is primary or that it takes some kind of precedence over the "open-choice" mode.

To answer this question, one would need a way of knowing to what extent a speaker relies on prefabricated formulas when producing language. At the moment there is no answer to this question. Of course, we could say that formulaic language is produced by recourse to the idiom principle, in which case the answer to the question would be the same: between one third and a half. However, maybe in the future other methods will provide an answer. One promising direction of research is the exploration of the prosody of formulaic language. As was mentioned above, Pawley and Syder in their discussion of "native-like fluency" noted that certain phrases were delivered faster than the normal speed and were relatively pause free. This aspect of formulaic language does not appear to be at the centre of attention, but there is some research evidence showing that prosodic evidence may provide a verification for the formulaicity of word sequences (Lin, 2012; Lin & Adolphs, 2009). There is also the possibility that eventually research into brain activity will throw more light on the picture, as the processing of formulaic and non-formulaic language has been connected to different parts of the brain.

7.3.2. THEORETICAL SUPPORT FOR THE FORMULAIC NATURE OF LANGUAGE PROCESSING

At this point one could ask if the dual models presented above are based on pure speculation, or if there is empirical evidence to support them. The criticism made by Myles and Cordier about the confusion of speaker-internal and external aspects of formulaicity has to do with the fact that many researchers "take as their basis what usually happens in the language surrounding the speaker, extrapolating that this preferential status has consequences for the storage of these sequences in the speakers of that language" (Myles & Cordier, 2016, p. 4). In other words, it is somehow taken for granted that manifestations of formulaicity in language production do have an underlying psycholinguistic reality, as in the "dual" models mentioned above.

Even though they do have a point in that such a connection is indeed often assumed or taken for granted without sufficient proof, there is substantial theoretical and empirical evidence to support the connection between formulaicity observed in language and the postulated formulaic nature of language processing.

First of all, the formulaic nature of language processing is supported by theories of chunking. The process of chunking, a phenomenon described by psychologists (Chase, W. G., & Simon, 1973; Gobet et al., 2001), is believed to take place at all levels of language (Nation, 2001, p. 319), enabling the grouping of smaller units into larger wholes. For example, morphemes are processed as units, not as sequences of phonemes, and complex words are likewise processed in their entirety, rather than as combinations of individual morphemes. The fact that chunking takes place does not preclude the possibility of the analysis of wholes into parts if the need arises. Thus the purpose of chunking is to give a processing advantage, enabling language comprehension and production at a greater speed (N. C. Ellis, 2003). At the same time, chunks need to be separately stored, alongside individual items (Nation, 2001, pp. 320–321). The concept of a "chunk" implies that a multi-word combination is stored just like an individual word, or, at least, that the constituent items of the chunk are recalled and produced in a certain linear order. However, as Weinert (1995, p. 197) suggests, there is no reason to believe that all kinds of formulaic chunks are stored in the same way. Indeed, there is no clarity as to what chunking is, when it comes to language, technically speaking. Wray (2012, pp. 233–234) asks the important question

> … of whether a processing advantage in terms of speed indicates holistic storage or simply the faster mapping of components – and indeed whether these are really two different things or just different ways of conceptualizing the same thing. The notion of holistic

storage could be viewed as a device for talking about linguistic units
that are ring-fenced for speedy processing – at the level of articula-
tion, this must presumably be the case. On the other hand, there is
potentially a different quality to holistic storage and access. First,
it could entail the synchronous access of all components (...). Second, it could entail accessing (albeit in sequence) larger base components, through a direct mapping from the meaning of the entire
expression to the phonological form (of those parts that are reliably
fixed – as construction models might favour). Third, in the case of
word strings that have become fused through repeated use, it could
entail the creation of a new access pathway that bypasses the original componential route – as the extensive neurological research into
automatic processing indicates.

Hoey's concept of "lexical priming" (2005) is based on the idea that
lexical patterns are responsible for the structure of language: "as
a word is acquired through encounters with it in speech and writing, it becomes cumulatively loaded with the contexts and co-texts
in which it is encountered, and our knowledge of it includes the fact
that it co-occurs with certain other words in certain kinds of context" (Hoey, 2005, p. 8). It is priming, then, that enables recurrent
co-occurrence of words; syntax, therefore, is merely an outcome of
the pervasiveness of collocation.

7.3.3. EMPIRICAL EVIDENCE SUPPORTING THE FORMULAIC
NATURE OF LANGUAGE PROCESSING IN NATIVE SPEAKERS

Even though some scholars argue that there is no sufficient evidence
of the psychological reality of the idiom principle (Siyanova-Chanturia & Martinez, 2015), there is in fact substantial evidence confirming the existence of the formulaic mode of language processing.

Empirical evidence which suggests that multi-word units are stored as wholes comes mostly, though not exclusively, from research on the processing of idioms by native speakers. Conklin and Schmitt provide a review of studies on idioms which provide empirical evidence that "formulaic language is processed both more quickly and potentially differently from nonformulaic language" (2012, p. 47). Such studies are very numerous (too numerous to be listed here) but the general conclusion that emerges from this vast body of research is that idioms in general tend to be processed faster than comparable non-idiomatic sequences. This phenomenon has been observed both in studies which compared the processing times for the figurative and the literal interpretations of the same idioms, as well as ones which compared the processing of idioms and comparable non-idiomatic sequences. For example, in one of the early such studies, Van Lancker and colleagues (Van Lancker, Canter, & Terbeek, 1981) had participants read aloud sentences with phrases which can be read either literally or figuratively, such as "he didn't know he was skating on thin ice," and observed that the participants inserted longer pauses into the phrase when the sentence context required a literal interpretation, while running the words together if the context supported the idiomatic interpretation. Whether the idiom is decomposable or oblique – for example, *pop the question* vs. *kick the bucket* – does not make a difference, both of these types are processed faster than their non-idiomatic counterparts, for example, *ask the question* and *fill the bucket*, respectively (Tabossi, Fanari, & Wolf, 2009). This suggests that formulaicity in itself speeds up processing. However, as rightly pointed out by Conklin & Schmitt (2012), studies on idioms are not ideal for drawing conclusions about formulaic language in general, because idioms are special in many ways – they are marked, and they are sometimes relatively rare. This is why of even more interest are studies which examine the processing of formulaic language by native speakers in which the target expressions are less idiomatic, but simply frequent.

In a study by Bod from 2000 (quoted in Bod, Hay, & Jannedy, 2003) participants responded faster to three-word subject-verb-object sequences when they were frequent (for example, *I like it*) than when they had a lower frequency (as in the case of, for instance, *I keep it*). The sequences were otherwise matched for structure, level of complexity, as well as the lexical frequencies of the individual items. This was interpreted as suggesting holistic storage of the more frequent ones. A similar study by Arnon and Snider (2010) employed four-word phrases which are completely compositional and comprehensible, such as *don't have to worry*. Again, the components of those sequences were matched for length and frequency; it was only the frequencies of the entire phrases that were different. The results confirmed faster processing time for the more frequent sequences. This was interpreted as meaning that language users notice and store frequency information with respect not only to individual lexical items, but also with regard to multiword phrases, even entirely compositional ones. Another interesting study (Tremblay, Derwing, Libben, & Westbury, 2011) compared the speed with which the participants read two versions of a passage: one containing lexical bundles (such as *don't worry about it*), and the other comparable non-bundle strings. The results showed that the passages with the bundles were read faster, and they were also better remembered and recalled more correctly than the passages which contained ordinary word combinations. Those findings were corroborated by a study using a different methodology, namely phrase recall and electrophysiological (ERP) measures (Tremblay & Baayen, 2010). They focused on phrases such as *in the middle of*, and found that their frequencies correlated with the participants' recall. Sosa and MacFarlane (2002) tested reaction times to phrases with different frequencies, all containing the word *of*. The authors observed a clear correlation between the frequencies and the reaction times, which they interpreted as indicating holistic storage.

There are also studies in which lexical bundles are the specific type of formulaic language under investigation (Nekrasova, 2009; Schmitt, Grandage, & Adolphs, 2004). Schmitt and his colleagues used a dictation task in which the participants are presented with longer stretches of dictated language than normally one's short-term memory can hold. Some of the dictated stretches had formulaic items embedded in them, some did not. The idea was that the participants would have to reconstruct the strings, so they would recall them imperfectly, but the embedded formulaic phrases were expected to be rendered more accurately than the rest of the dictated text, possibly without pauses and hesitations, which would be interpreted as evidence of their holistic storage. This hypothesis was only partly supported, with some formulaic sequences being recalled intact by some speakers. This raises the possibility that either the frequency of occurrence in language is not directly related to which phrases are stored holistically, or there may be variability from speaker to speaker with respect to which phrases are stored as chunks. However, as Nekrasova (2009) pointed out, the formulaic phrases embedded in the study by Schmitt and colleagues were of many different types. Some did and some did not have a pragmatic function, some were more typical of conversation, some were more academic, and they varied greatly in terms of frequency, which may explain the inconclusive results.

A very important fact which should be noted at this stage is that all the studies mentioned above, except for the ones involving idioms, used the frequencies of the entire phrases as the measure of formulaicity. However, it has been suggested that formulaicity may be related not only to the raw frequencies of strings, but also to measures of the exclusivity of the co-occurrence of the constituent elements of a string. As was mentioned above, one such measure is the MI (mutual information) score. Indeed, it seems reasonable that MI may be related to the psycholinguistic status of some phrases. As Gablasova, Brezina and McEnery (2017, p. 160) explain:

Exclusivity is likely to be strongly linked to predictability of co-occurrence, when the appearance of one part of the collocation brings
to mind the other part. For example, collocations such as *zig zag*,
okey dokey, and *annus mirrabilis* are fairly exclusively associated. We
could hypothesize that words that are likely to be seen in each other's company may be more easily recognized, acquired, and stored
as a unit.

Another source of support for the existence of formulaic processing
of language comes from studies involving patients with brain damage (Van Lancker-Sidtis & Postman, 2006; Van Lancker & Kempler,
1987; Van Lancker Sidtis, 2012). It appears that the representation of
familiar phrases (idioms, collocations, routines, *etc.*) in the brain may
be different from that of non-formulaic language, and that the two
types of language may differ with respect to lateralization: the results
suggest that novel language is processed in the left hemisphere, while
formulaic language in the right one.

Another line of inquiry which offers support for the co-existence
of formulaic and non-formulaic processing of language can be found
in studies on the prosody of formulaic language. Lin (2012) argues
for the potential of prosodic features to identify formulaic phrases,
and mentions a number of studies which point to the association of
formulaic phrases with certain prosodic features, specific stress patterns, specific alignment of pauses, and the faster speed and rhythm
of speech (Kuiper, 2004). Further support for this position is provided
by Hallin and Van Lancker Sidtis (2017), who compared the prosodic
characteristics of naturally spoken Swedish sentences with proverbs
and matched control sentences. The sentences with proverbs were
spoken differently, both in terms of speed and tonal pattern. The distinctive prosodic characteristics of the formulaic parts of sentences
were interpreted by the authors as suggesting holistic storage for formulaic sequences, supporting in general the dual process of language

competence. The authors also provide a tentative suggestion concerning the neurolinguistic reality behind formulaic language, suggesting that formulaic expressions are stored and processed as complex motor gestures, modulated by subcortical motor systems, in which a key role is played by the basal ganglia (Hallin & Van Lancker Sidtis, 2017). As they say, "the dual-process model proposes that formulaic expressions are produced using holistically stored motoric gestures modulated by a right hemisphere-subcortical system. A holistically stored motoric gesture can be expected to be produced with a faster rate than a composed one" (Hallin & Van Lancker Sidtis, 2017, p. 85). This would explain why patients with damage to the basal ganglia suffer an impoverishment of formulaic language.

All in all, the available research seems to strongly support the view that there exists a formulaic mode for the processing of language, and, very importantly, for formulaic language other than idioms, the researchers have established a connection between the frequency of phrases and the speed or ease of processing. In other words, the more frequent a phrase is, the more likely it is to be processed as a chunk. At the same time, processing advantages are also observed for formulaic language which is not necessarily frequent, but fixed (such as idioms), which means that the token frequency of certain phrases is not the only predictor of formulaic processing.

7.4. FORMULAICITY, FREQUENCY AND RECENT TRENDS IN LINGUISTICS

The research reviewed above – especially the fact that frequency effects are observed for decomposable, transparent but frequent sequences – ties in with a number of linguistic theories which blur the distinction between grammar and lexis. As far as English linguistics is concerned, the concepts of lexis and grammar being interconnected can be seen as going back to Halliday (1961). Later on, corpus linguistics provided extensive support for the recognition of the ubiquitous nature of formulaicity in language. More recently, the recognition of the role of frequency has chimed very well with usage-based models of language (Bybee, 2006, 2007; Bybee & Hopper, 2001; Goldberg, 2006; Langacker, 1987, 2000; MacWhinney, 2006; Tomasello, 2003).

Those models emphasise the data-driven nature of learning, seeing it as a process driven by experience. In section 4.3, it was said that learning can be seen as an unconscious, automatic, frequency-based process of induction (N. C. Ellis, 2005). As the result of coming in contact with samples of language, certain form-meaning mappings become gradually automatic for a given speaker. Related terms used to refer to this process are *entrenchment* (Langacker, 1987) and *automaticity* (Segalowitz, 2003). In usage-based models, learning is inductive. Since exposure to input is the reason why people acquire language, it naturally follows that the more frequently a certain structure is encountered, the more likely it is to become entrenched. Entrenchment is thus related to the frequency of occurrence of specific items in the language.

In the school of linguistic thought known as construction grammar (Goldberg, 2006; Tomasello, 2003), the language learner acquires a set of constructions as a result of repeated experiences. These constructions may be of different sizes as well as levels of abstractness. Many different factors may interplay with the acquisition of constructions; however, the most important variable at play is frequency (see e.g. Gries & Ellis, 2015). Depending on the frequency with which a particular linguistic construction is encountered, it becomes represented in the lexicon with weaker or stronger connections. Again, the language appears to be an accumulation of experiences, which changes every time (even if only to a minute extent) every time a new sample of language is encountered.

Those models tie in with the theory that the primary language learning mechanism is statistical learning (which was already briefly mentioned in section 4.3). This view holds that humans are sensitive to frequencies of co-occurrence, and, without being consciously aware of it, they accumulate this frequency information until patterns of grammatical structure emerge (Rebuschat & Williams, 2012; Rebuschat et al., 2012). Learning is thus seen as "a gradual process of accumulating linguistic knowledge based on the distributional properties of the input" (Andringa & Rebuschat, 2015, p. 188). It has to be noted, though, that the discovery of patterns in the input, such as the transitional probability between adjacent elements, has been investigated mostly in infants, in L1 contexts (see Romberg & Saffran, 2010), and the exact nature of statistical learning remains unknown, with one likely possibility being chunk formation (Hamrick, 2014).

Those theories are compatible with connectionist approaches (Rumelhart & McClelland, 1986) to language processing (for an illuminating overview and discussion, see Singleton, 1999). The connectionist paradigm "sees knowledge in terms of soft connection strength rather than rules or patterns" (Singleton, 1999, p. 123). The concept of spreading activation and parallel processing are compatible with views which emphasize statistical properties of the input in language learning (Chater & Manning, 2006).

A related line of inquiry is the application of probabilistic models to language acquisition and processing. Chater and Manning (2006) provide an in-depth discussion of those models and argue that, with recent advances in the field, probabilistic models can now account for the learning and processing of language, and that learning a language involves learning probabilistic models (Chater & Manning, 2006). Those models can thus provide a theoretical base for explaining how learners acquire language through sensitivity to the frequencies of patterns in the input.

7.5. FORMULAIC LANGUAGE IN L2 SPEAKERS

All of the studies mentioned in the above section involved native speakers, and most of them involved only native speakers. This section looks at the available information concerning formulaic language in L2 learners. For the sake of clarity, it will first look at "speaker-external" data, and will then look at attempts to investigate the "speaker-internal" aspects.

7.5.1. SPEAKER-EXTERNAL ASPECTS

The best-known fact about formulaic language and L2 learners is that it usually appears to be insufficiently developed. There seems to be a consensus as to the fact that "formulaicity (...) is an area where second language (L2) learners only very slowly close the gap on native speakers" (Boers & Lindstromberg, 2012, p. 83). In a study that investigated the use of one type of formulaic language – namely collocations – by L2 learners, Laufer and Waldman (2011) found that L2 learners at all proficiency levels produce fewer collocations than native speakers, errors in collocation use persist even at high level of advancement, and it is only at the relatively advanced stages of L2 learning that the number of collocations increases in learners' language. Collocations are well documented as a problem area even for advanced learners: "even advanced learners have considerable difficulties in the production of collocations" (Nesselhauf, 2003, p. 237); "Thus, for advanced students collocations present a major problem in the production of correct English" (Bahns & Eldaw, 1993, p. 101).

A number of studies provide the finding that the use of formulaic language by language learners is different from that of native speakers (e.g. Granger, 1998). L2 learners are known to be unaware of some typical phrases, and tend to put words together on the basis of their individual meaning, which accounts for the "foreign-soundingness" of L2 learners' language. Learners' collocational choices are also likely to be affected by their L1 (Leśniewska, 2003; Singleton, Leśniewska, & Witalisz, 2007; Yamashita & Jiang, 2010).

The use of collocations in a second language also tends to be very limited, and influenced by frequency in the language. To that effect, a study of collocations in L2 learners (Durrant & Schmitt, 2009) showed that L2 learners indeed use collocations, but only certain types; namely, they rely heavily on high-frequency collocations, while underusing certain collocations that would better express the meaning intended, but that are less frequent in English.

7.5.2. SPEAKER-INTERNAL ASPECTS

Two very different possibilities are entertained in the literature as far as the use of formulaic language by L2 learners is concerned. One view is that L2 learners (as opposed to child L1 learners) may be taking a non-formulaic approach to learning a language (Wray, 2002a). In this view, learners are much more likely to focus on individual words.

> The adult language learner, on encountering major catastrophe, would break it down into a word meaning "big" and a word meaning "disaster" and store the words separately, without any information about the fact that they went together. When the need arose in the future to express the idea again, they would have no memory of major catastrophe as the pairing originally encountered, and any pairing of words with the right meaning would seem equally plausible.
>
> (Wray, 2002a, p. 209)

This stands to reason, and is supported both by research (such as that mentioned in the above section) and plenty of anecdotal evidence. Differences in the use of formulaic expressions between L1 and L2 speakers are well documented, and language learners often sound unidiomatic. In this view, efforts to learn idiomatic expressions made at higher level of advancement are just the icing on the cake, rather than being a basis of all learning, as is the case with L1 learners, especially as seen by usage-based models.

Another view is that the mechanisms central to the usage-based models of learning, statistical, probability-driven learning, determined by the frequency of forms in the input, may also be applicable to L2 acquisition (N. C. Ellis, 2003). Some authors like to view those two possibilities as contradictory and mutually incompatible (see e.g. Durrant & Schmitt, 2009). For example, Conklin and Schmitt ask:

> If native speakers are able to decrease demands on cognitive capacity because formulaic sequences are, in a sense, ready to go, are non-native speakers able to do the same? This is an important issue, as some evidence seems to show that second language (L2) learners neglect phrases, focusing instead on individual words.
>
> (Conklin & Schmitt, 2012, pp. 45–46)

The authors thus address the potential use or non-use of formulaic sequences by non-native speakers as a dichotomous issue, which may not be entirely justified. Cognitive behaviour usually shows high variation across individuals, and within the same individual across levels of L2 proficiency. Consequently, the amount of reliance on formulaicity may vary greatly from learner to learner, and within each individual as well.

Two main reasons could explain why the research on the processing of formulaic language by L2 learners is not likely to make significant advances: (1) various processes in L2 learners may well coexist;

and (2) it makes little sense to consider language learners as a group with shared characteristics, because of the wealth of different factors involved, among which one of the most important ones is the level of proficiency. This would explain why there is both evidence pointing to the non-formulaic nature of learners' production, as was briefly presented above, and why there is quite a lot of empirical support for the fact that formulaicity does play a role in L2 use, as will be shown below.

RESEARCH FINDINGS SUPPORTING FORMULAIC PROCESSING IN L2

While it is known that language users are sensitive to frequency effects in their L1, it is only recently that this issue has been investigated with respect to L2 acquisition and use. The most common means of investigating frequency effects is by testing whether response times in online lexical decision tasks vary depending on the frequency of the stimulus word in the language. Durrant and Schmitt found that adult learners do retain information about the co-occurrence of specific words in the input (Durrant & Schmitt, 2010), which they interpreted as undermining the belief that the L2 use is "non-formulaic."

A study by Siyanova-Chanturia, Conklin, and van Heuven (2011) employed eye-tracking methodology to investigate processing by native and non-native English speakers of sentences including formulaic sequences with different frequencies, more specifically, three-word binomials such as *bride and groom* and their inverted versions (*groom and bride*), which provided excellent controls because they were identical in all respects (syntax, meaning, frequency of constituent items) except the frequency of the entire binomial. The more frequent versions of the binomials were read faster, both by native and non-native speakers. The impact of input frequency on processing time was also demonstrated by Jiang and Nekrasova (2007) in a study involving grammaticality judgements made by L2 speakers. The researchers observed that those judgements were faster and more accurate than for control strings which were not formulaic. Likewise, Wolter and Gyllstad (2013) found that advanced learners of English show sensitivity to frequency effects with respect to collocations.

LEVEL OF PROFICIENCY

Interestingly, it seems that proficiency level of the learners plays a major role in their sensitivity to frequency effects, which is perfectly in keeping with commonsensical expectations, since sensitivity to frequency effects comes from exposure to language, and that exposure increases as the learners make progress. In the above-mentioned study by Siyanova-Chanturia, Conklin, and van Heuven (2011) observed sensitivity to frequency effects in both native speakers and advanced non-native speakers, but not for intermediate learners. Wolter and Yamashita (2018) found that in both native speakers, as well as lower level and higher level learners of English, the speed of processing of collocations depends on both the frequency of individual components and the frequencies of the whole collocation, but the proportions to which those factors influence the response times varies depending on the proficiency level. The authors observed "a shift away from reliance on word-level frequency to collocational frequency that occurred with gains in proficiency" (Wolter & Yamashita, 2018, p. 441). The two studies mentioned earlier in and Schmitt and colleagues (Schmitt et al., 2004), apart from native speakers also included non-native speakers, and found that non-natives become better at accurately producing lexical bundles as their proficiency increases.

FORMULAS AS AN AID

Formulaic language may be seen as a learning strategy in L2 acquisition: learners may memorise chunks, use them as wholes, and eventually derive rules for productive use. Learners may also use chunks which enable them to function in a specific situation, in which case the chunks play a specific pragmatic role and enable communication. There is a certain similarity in the role of chunks in L1 and L2 acquisition: in both cases the chunks may contain language which is more syntactically complex than the current ability of the learner allows for in free production, or it may contain vocabulary items which the learner is unable to use correctly outside of the chunk. Apart from this similarity, however, making comparisons between L1 and L2 use of chunks is risky, nor is it justified to draw any conclusions about the role of chunks in L2 acquisition on the basis of L1 acquisition, as the two processes may be essentially different, due to differences in cognitive processing between infants acquiring the L1 and L2 learners, who may be of any age.

Learners "always feel pressure to produce more than they can" (Nattinger & DeCarrico, 1992, p. 27), and prefabricated patterns enable them "to express functions which they are yet unable to construct from their linguistic system" (Hakuta, 1976, p. 333). The role of formulaic language in language production is discussed, among others, by Raupach (1984), who shows that advanced L2 learners make use of formulas in their speech, mostly as fluency devices and discourse organizers. Raupach also demonstrates that L2 learners use their own formulas, which may or may not correspond to target language formulas. Some target language formulas are overused, and some are underused by learners. Towell, Hawkins and Bazergui (1996) carried out a longitudinal study comparing learners of French before and after they stayed in a French-speaking country, and attributed the resulting increase in the fluency to the proceduralisation of knowledge, that is, to the fact that the learners stored memorized sequences of language. The observation was made on the basis of counting the mean length of run (number of successive syllables unbroken by a pause) and other characteristics of the learners' speech. Dechert (1983) examined the language production of a German learner of English, and that learner proved more fluent when formulaic language was used.

This kind of facilitating effect of collocational knowledge in learners (making it easier to use articles, prepositions, *etc.*) has also been treated as a compensatory strategy, even though this view is not common. An example is provided by a study by Mueller (2011), who tested advanced adult English learners with different L1s on their ability to fill in a gapped test in which prepositions had been removed. The study is carried out on the basis of the assumption that "collocational knowledge may serve a compensatory role" (Mueller, 2011, p. 480). The author observes that "second language learners' interlanguage relies on collocational knowledge in lieu of precise semantic knowledge" (p. 480). This position sees an element of the target language competence (in this particular case, the command of prepositions) as being produced by native speakers thanks to "precise semantic knowledge." Learners, who lack that knowledge, may rely on the compensatory strategy of relying on remembered collocations. This view does not seem particularly convincing: the whole power of collocational associations between words is seen as merely an intermediate step on the way to full mastery of language.

DO CHUNKS FEED INTO RULES?

There exists an important difference between L1 and L2 learners with respect to acquisition. Chunks are known to play an important role in child L1 acquisition, being acquired as wholes and only later broken up into constituent parts (Brown, 1973; Peters, 1983; Wong-Fillmore, 1976).

As to whether or not this happens in L2 learning, opinions and research findings are mixed. Some researchers say that the roles formulas play in the development of rules is negligible. An early review by Weinert (1995) arrived at this conclusion: the use of formulas does not contribute to the subsequent grammatical development in the L2. Yorio (1989, p. 68) concluded that adult L2 learners "do not appear to make extensive early use of prefabricated, formulaic language, and when they do, they do not appear to be able to use it to further their grammatical development." Similarly, Wray (2002b, p. 116) suggests that the formulaic mode of processing "tends to be avoided – with some disadvantageous consequences – during post-childhood second-language learning."

In contrast, Bolander (1989) gave evidence of the presence of formulaic speech in the language production of tutored adult learners of Swedish as a second language. The use of "formula-like clauses" was found to promote the application of syntactic rules, such as inversion and the placement of the negative particle in Swedish. Formulas were identified as

> different types of frequent combinations of words constituting various parts of sentences, that appear to be used as ready-made units in processing... The criterion for regarding a sequence as a chunk/prefab is the learners' manifestation of them as such in their speech, as shown either by a more frequent than average correct production of a certain structure, or by errors in structures that are otherwise correct.
>
> (Bolander, 1989, p. 73)

Bolander also gave one suggestion as to how prefabs could lead to the formulation of rules: "... when the number of prefabs stored in memory is large enough, syntactic rules are derived as help for the memory to economize and rationalize processing" (Bolander, 1989, p. 85). Similar conclusions were drawn by Myles, Hooper and Mitchell (1998), who found that formulas in the acquisition of French as L2 facilitated communication, accelerated production in the early stages, and also contributed to the acquisition of grammatical rules.

PROSODY

Going back to the connection between formulaic language and prosody (discussed in 7.3.3.), Lin (2012) argues that prosody might be more than just a characteristic feature of formulaic language. It may be that "prosody underlies the mechanism by which we learn and remember formulaic language" (Lin, 2012, p. 343). The main point raised by Lin (2012) is that prosody is likely to play a key role in formulaic language.

Lin (2012) looked at a study by Peters (Peters, 1977), who – according to Lin – was the first researcher to notice that children can produce chunks that are more complex than their current stage of development would allow for. Also, importantly, some utterances produced by young children, despite their low phonemic accuracy, have a distinctive melody which resembles the sound of those chunks in adult speech. Lin interprets this as meaning that "prosody takes precedence in children's acquisition of formulaic language" (2012, p. 344), which means that it is possible that "the prosodic form of the chunks is the primary form that is stored in every entry of the formulaic chunks" (2012, p. 344).

Lin writes that this is essentially bad news for language learners, because of the "relative poverty of spontaneous spoken input" (2012, p. 344). She specifically has in mind the English language learners in China. However, even if the input were just as rich as that of L1 learners, the presence of developed cognition and literacy in L2 learners means that the processes have to be different. Literacy has a particularly important role, as traditionally words are represented as individual entities separated by spaces, which encourages their perception as units, whereas in speech word boundaries are not really perceptible.

7.6. FORMULAICITY AND SECOND LANGUAGE TEACHING: A BRIEF HISTORY

Very broadly speaking, the beginnings of the field of second language acquisition research were characterized by a focus on grammar. For quite a long time, it seemed that vocabulary was a relatively neglected area. What followed was a quick growth of interest in the lexical aspects of L2 learning and teaching in the 1990s. At the turn of the millennium, a new topic of interest began to emerge in second language acquisition research: collocations. Personally, when I first researched the topic of collocations in the first years of this century, there was still only a handful of (mostly very recent) research studies which referred to this concept. In the literature on language teaching, there was no trace of that term, and a thorough search in the indices of language teaching methodology handbooks available in the early 2000s revealed that the term was never discussed (Leśniewska, 2003). The *Oxford Collocations Dictionary* (2002) intended for learners of English, was first published in 2002. The beginnings of the 21st century also saw a growing interest in advanced levels of L2 proficiency, including near-native levels, which brought into focus the collocational aspects of language competence (Howarth, 1996; Nesselhauf, 2003).

For the sake of the historical record, it should be noted that, while none of the major publishing houses of ELT textbooks and dictionaries had any materials on collocations in the 20th century, there were some notable exceptions. A set of very collocation-focused textbooks of English was published in London by Macmillan by a Polish linguist, Brygida Rudzka, and her colleagues (Rudzka, Channell, Putseys, & Ostyn, 1981, 1985). There was a small dictionary of collocations published by John Benjamins (Benson, Benson, & Ilson, 1986). In Poland, a dictionary with selected English collocations was published at roughly the same time (Douglas Kozłowska & Dzierżanowska, 1988).

In the last decade, the picture changed completely. Dictionaries of English have begun to include increasing amounts of collocational information, and activities explicitly addressing collocations are now a standard feature of ELT materials.

7.7. ARTICLES AND FORMULAICITY

As could be seen in Chapter 5, the assumption behind the vast majority of studies on articles carried out so far is that articles are indeed form-function relations, but very complex ones. Virtually the entire body of research on articles deals with the issue from the perspective of grammar. It seems that, to date, researchers have not explored the use of articles in L2 English from the perspective of formulaicity, with one exception, which is very relevant for this study: a corpus-based study by Leńko-Szymańska (2012). Leńko-Szymańska looked at the use of the definite article in the 3-grams found in a corpus of ESL learner writing, and compared it to that in a native corpus. The 3-grams, that is, three-word lexical bundles, included items such as *one of the, go to the, part of the, there is a, he was a, there is a.* One very interesting finding which emerged from this study is that, in 3-grams, the definite article occurs much more often (ca. 30% of the uses) than the indefinite article (ca. 17% of the uses). In the learner data, *the* also occurs more often in bundles than *a/an*, across all levels of proficiency. A corpus approach like this one has some limitations, however: it does not take into consideration correctness – some, probably many, uses of articles in the learner corpus may be incorrect; it does not provide any data about the use of the zero article. However, this approach has the benefit of clearly showing how the use of articles in lexical bundles becomes more frequent as proficiency increases. In fact, at advanced levels, the frequency in the use of the definite article in bundles by L2 learners reaches that of native speakers, and for the indefinite article it is actually higher than the native norm. At the same time, the rule-based uses of articles fall below the native norm, even at the advanced level. This finding is extremely interesting, as it suggests that there may be a phraseological effect at play affecting the way learners of English use articles, since articles are more likely to be used by learners if they are part of a frequent combination of words.

Of particular importance is the fact that most of the existing studies on articles not only do not deal with formulaic aspects, but also actually exclude any conventional uses of articles from their analysis. Such studies may acknowledge the fact that some uses of articles are motivated by convention rather than by the referentiality and specificity of a given NP, but they actually take pains to omit such conventional or idiomatic uses from their results (Butler, 2002; Díez-Bedmar & Papp, 2008) or the discussion (Thomas, 1989), which is understandable, since they are not the focus of those analyses. There are some rare exceptions to this general approach: for example, Thomas (1989) remarks that a high level of accuracy observed for one particular use of the indefinite article in the [+SR –HK] context could be attributed to the learners acquiring the structure *there is a/an* as a single chunk.

Idiomatic uses of articles were included in the studies by Ekiert (2004) and Li and Yang (2010) and the ability to use a/an develops earlier than the ability to use "zero article" Ø. These findings help us understand why lower-intermediate and intermediate learners tend to overuse the and a/an and underuse Ø, while advanced learners often overuse Ø. For intermediate Chinese learners of English, tasks that require them to choose articles before generic nouns ([−SR, +HK], with Polish and Chinese learners, respectively. The authors elicited article choices by means of a gap-filling test. The tested items included such expressions as *game of Ø cat and Ø mouse, getting Ø cold feet,* or *thrown out of Ø work.* The results showed that the idiomatic use of articles, understood in this way, is problematic for both groups of learners.

In view of the growing recognition of the fact that language processing is formulaic to a considerable extent, as reviewed above, it stands to reason that the use of articles in English may also to some extent rely on formulaicity-related mechanisms. Even those uses of articles which appear to be rule-governed (i.e., syntactically regular) may in fact be aided by the mechanisms which are responsible for formulaicity in language use. This possibility will be explored in Chapter 8.

7.8. CONCLUSIONS

The nature of language production can be accounted for in terms of syntactic rules, on the one hand, and the retrieval of formulaic language, which can also be broken down into component parts if there is need to do so, on the other. The role of formulaic language is explained by the economics of language production: it represents a compromise between increased demands on storage space and gains in the speed of production and ease of comprehension. It is now well established that native speakers process various types of formulaic language in a way that offers an advantage over individual word selection. Those findings fit in well with current developments in recent developments in linguistics and psychology, such as usage-based grammars, and models which emphasise probabilistic and statistical learning. It is known that frequency of occurrence of specific word strings corresponds to the likelihood of the string being processed in a formulaic manner, even though what formulaic processing technically means exactly is not yet entirely clear.

The research findings are less clear with respect to L2 learners, but all in all indicate that L2 learners are sensitive to frequency of word combinations in the input, and that sensitivity improves with the level of advancement.

Therefore, it seems that the conclusion of Conklin and Schmitt seems fully justified:

> [A]dult native speakers, and most likely children and non-native speakers who have had enough exposure to a language, appear to have representations not only for the words that make up formulaic sequences (fish, and, chips) but also for the sequence itself (fish and chips). Frequency seems to lead to a particular form being represented in the mental lexicon. However, if a form has not been encountered frequently enough, as in the case of lower proficiency non-native speakers or very young children, it appears that it may not be well entrenched in memory.
>
> (Conklin & Schmitt, 2012, p. 54)

Taking the above into consideration, it seems reasonable to assume that formulaicity is related to the frequency of occurrence, even though the exact nature of this connection has not been fully elucidated yet.

CHAPTER 8

Investigating article use
by advanced Polish learners of EFL:
The role of formulaicity

8.1. INTRODUCTION

This chapter presents an inquiry into the phraseological aspects of article use. As has been shown so far, there is extensive theoretical support in the literature for the idea that language use is to a considerable degree phraseologically motivated, and some empirical evidence has already accumulated which corroborates this view. It has also been shown that linguistic attempts to capture the functioning of the English articles in the form of rules are not only extremely complex, but they have relatively little predictive power, which negatively impacts their usability in English language teaching. In view of the overwhelming number of rules pertaining to article use and the apparent contradictions between them, it stands to reason that some facilitating mechanism may be playing a role in the correct use of articles, both for native and non-native speakers. As language users rely to a significant extent on the partly automatized retrieval of some word combinations, and articles are part of those word combinations, it is possible that making correct article choices is aided by the "idiom principle." This would hold true even when the use of an article can be explained by reference to a specific grammatical rule.

This chapter presents two investigations which put this hypothetical possibility to the test, bringing together the research I have conducted on the topic and showing the development of my methodological approach to investigating the issue. The first study reported here has been published previously (Leśniewska, 2016). For that reason, this chapter includes sections of text that are reproduced from the original article: section 8.2.1 on the participants, section 8.2.2 on the instruments and the procedure, and section 8.2.3 on the analysis, results and discussion.

8.1.1. PURPOSE AND RATIONALE

As could be seen in Chapter 5, studies on articles in L2 English are numerous, but the assumption which underlies most of them is that articles are rule-governed. This perspective is largely justified, as the English article system is indeed based on the key notions of definiteness, specificity and genericity, as well as on the countability and number of nouns, and on the distinction between proper and common nouns. However, the rules provided never account for the totality of article uses in natural language, as was demonstrated in Chapters 2 and 3.

This chapter presents an enquiry into the possibility that there is yet another perspective which may complement the existing picture of article use, namely a phraseological one. In other words, the research included here is an attempt at examining if the correct use of articles by language learners is to some extent aided by the mechanisms that underlie the formulaic character of language. It is important to stress that the focus here is on the possibility that formulaic "bonds" complement, or further strengthen, the use of articles in those contexts which are compliant with the "rules."

It is also important to note that the role of formulaicity which is hypothesised in this study is crucially different from the role usually assigned to phraseological aspects in descriptions of article use. Formulaicity is usually called upon to account for those uses of articles which somehow do not conform to the rules. For example, the use of articles in expressions such as *make a start, in a hurry, on loan, out of action* are in ESL materials explained as "idiomatic," which means that the learner should memorise them rather than try to apply any of the rules on article use. As we can read in a popular pedagogical grammar: "In a lot of idiomatic expressions articles are used or left out for no apparent reason other than they belong or don't belong in the expression. Learners need to learn these like items of vocabulary, and have to remember the whole phrase, ignoring general rules or sub-rules" (Parrott, 2000, p. 50). For example, if we take the English idiomatic expression *dog eat dog* and see it from the perspective of a learner of English, it is understandable that the learner needs to suppress the need to make the expression grammatically regular by adding articles and the third person-s ending to the noun (*a dog eats a dog*) or making the nouns plural (*dogs eat dogs*). It is thus a case of a clash between grammatical rules and the overriding, phraseological rule. In this study, however, I am concerned not with situations where the two are in conflict, but with those when the grammatical rules and the phraseological binding coincide, the idea being that the latter aids the former. For example, in the phrase *for the first time* the use of *the* is regular, but it may still be easier for the learner to make that correct choice and use the definite article in this phrase because the entire combination of words is to some extent familiar in its entirety (that is, it is formulaic).

8.1.2. APPROACH

Since it is assumed that formulaicity is related to frequency of use (as was discussed in Chapter 7), it follows that frequent word combinations are more formulaic than rare ones, all other things being equal. The studies presented below utilize this assumption in their design. Both feature research tools which allow for a comparison of the participants' use of articles in two types of contexts, comparable in all ways except for their level of formulaicity. This will allow to check the prediction that the participants' success in using articles will be greater in the more formulaic of two otherwise comparable contexts. The research tools used in both studies were designed specifically for this purpose, as no similar research seems to have been carried out.

8.2. STUDY 1

8.2.1. PARTICIPANTS

The participants in that first study were 90 Polish university students majoring in English language or linguistics. All were adult learners of English placed at the B2/C1 level in the Common European Framework of Reference for Languages (CEFR) (Council of Europe, 2011). The learners' L1 was Polish, an article-less language.

The learners had a specific profile: they had been learning English in a predominantly instructional context. As opposed to studies which involve ESL in immigrant settings, the learners in this study were unlikely to function socially or professionally in English in their everyday lives. This is relevant insofar as the instruction they had received as far as articles are concerned is extremely likely to have included metalinguistic explanation and focus-on-form type of teaching, just because of the general characteristics of the English courses taught at Polish schools.

The level of advancement of the students was assumed to be reflected in their placement in groups for their practical English classes. This general indication of the level of proficiency was considered sufficient for the purpose of this study. The first group ($n = 44$) gathered students whose level of English corresponded to the B2 level on the CEFR. The level of ESL proficiency of the second, more advanced group ($n = 46$) corresponded to the C1 level. All participants were between 20 and 22 years of age, with the mean age being slightly lower in Group 1.

8.2.2. INSTRUMENT AND PROCEDURE

The basic idea for the research instrument was to create a test in which the participants would have to supply missing articles in contexts which feature different levels of formulaicity. The test would thus include a number of obligatory occasions for the use of the definite article. Those occasions would be of two kinds: in some, the sequence of words requiring an article would be a frequently occurring combination, in some, it would be a novel combination of words, characterized by low frequency of occurrence. In other respects, the pairs of test items (high frequency item – low frequency item) would be as comparable as possible.

The one-page test used in this study (see Appendix 1) consisted of sentences in English from which all the articles had been removed. The participants were asked to put in the missing articles in the right places. The tests included a total of 12 pairs of target items (presented in a mixed-up order) which included exactly the same structures with articles: the definite, the indefinite, or the zero article. The pairs were as follows:

Item A:	Item B:
1. *a friend of mine*	– *an acquaintance of mine*
2. *what a shame*	– *what a remarkable player*
3. *twice a day*	– *five times a semester*
4. *the sooner the better*	– *the smaller the pot, the more critical the problem*
5. *a cup of tea*	– *a spoonful of syrup*
6. *the day I die*	– *the food I brought*
7. *help the poor*	– *open to the insured*
8. *hit (someone) in the face*	– *cut in the hand*
9. *speak English*	– *learn Kurdish*
10. *get a job*	– *live in a luxury apartment*
11. *have kids*	– *eat carbohydrates*
12. *the centre of attention*	– *the ecology of waterways*

Grammatically speaking, the reason for the use of the article was identical in item A and B of each pair, that is, the same grammatical "rule" applied in both cases. For example, items 5A and 5B both represent partitive expressions (a type of phrasal quantifiers) used to impose countability on non-count nouns (Quirk & Greenbaum, 1973, p. 67). Items 10A and 10B are both examples of the use of the indefinite article with referents that can be classified as countable, indefinite, and non-specific (Downing & Locke, 1992, p. 429). However, the items differed in one important aspect: the article in version A was contained in a frequently occurring word combination, whereas version B was relatively more of an "open choice" type of word combination.

TEST PREPARATION

Test preparation relied on a combination of researcher intuition, native speaker judgements, and frequency measures from corpus examination. The most challenging step in the process was to find suitable word combination pairs which would qualify as, respectively, more "idiom-principle-driven" and more "open-choice" in character.

A brainstorm session between two linguistics researchers aimed at identifying pairs of word combinations that were perceived by the researchers as being more typical and frequent, versus more "open-choice" combinations. Intuitive ratings thus formed the basis for the initial selection of word combination pairs. Those pairs were then submitted to two colleagues who are native speakers of English, which led to further elimination of pairs on which there was lack of inter-judge agreement, the replacement and changes to some word combinations, and a resulting group of 20 word-combination pairs.

The frequency of co-occurrence for those initial intuition-based pairings was verified using two corpora: the British National Corpus (Davies, 2004) and the Corpus of Contemporary American English (Davies, 2008), which will be referred to as BNC and COCA, respectively. Those corpora were deemed adequate due to their size (100 million and 450 million words, respectively) and representative character. The BNC is made up of written (90%) and spoken (10%) language, and contains texts from a wide range of sources (for example, different kinds of journals, periodicals, newspapers, academic books, popular fiction), in order to represent a wide cross-section of British English. The COCA is also a balanced corpus, made up of texts representing spoken language, fiction, popular magazines, newspapers, and academic texts.

While both corpora were used in the initial search in order to locate suitable pairs for the test, a specific threshold was set with reference to the COCA corpus, the frequency findings from which were considered more reliable because of its larger size. The frequent combination in each pair had to occur at least 40 times more often than its rare counterpart in order to be included in the test. The rare items had a frequency of 0.02 per million words or less, while the frequent items had a frequency of 0.18 or more. While it was impossible to determine a perfect set of criteria which could be applied if there was a way to extract the items automatically, this frequency requirement was considered to provide sufficient support for the intuitive judgements.

Not all intuition-based pairs corresponded to corpus-based frequency data, nor were frequency counts always similar in both corpora. Consequently, the 12 pairs which showed the most convincing difference in the frequency of occurrence were retained. The full list of items and frequencies is provided in Appendix 2.

The 12 pairs (24 target items) were presented hidden among other sentences in the test, which not only helped to provide more context for the target items, but also to make the relationship between the pairs of target items less noticeable. It should be noted that all the articles were removed from all the sentences included in the test. Only some of the missing articles in the test were the actual target items. Since all articles were removed, the number of missing articles was larger than the number of the target items under investigation.

For example, in the case of pair no. 3, which tested the use of the indefinite article in expressions of frequency, the more frequent of the two combinations, *twice a day*, appears in test item 7:

By midsummer, herbs and vegetables in containers may need water twice day.

Whereas its counterpart, the open-choice combination *five times a semester*, can be found in test item no. 4:

We meet regularly, five times semester, at departmental meeting.

The noun phrase *departmental meeting* also requires an article, but whether the participants inserted it or not was not taken into consideration, as this noun phrase was not one of the target items. Such missing articles outside the target items helped distract the test-takers from any pattern in the test design they might be able to discern.

An initial version of the test was piloted with three native and three non-native speakers of English to ensure that the removal of articles did not create ambiguous or incomprehensible sentences, as well as to check if, for all the target items, all the native speakers always provided the same response. The target items which did not meet this criterion were replaced. Variation in the native speakers' choices of articles in the test outside the target items was considered of no importance. Rare or difficult lexical items were avoided in the test. Care was taken to ensure that both the frequent and the rare combinations of words were composed of "ordinary," relatively frequent lexical items which are expected to be known to learners of English at the intermediate and higher levels. Two experienced teachers of English were consulted about the likelihood that all the words used on the test would be known by our target audience. Teachers were convinced that all items would be known by our test participants, and post-test conversations with a few participants confirmed that no lexical item on the test was new to them. Difficult words, due to their greater length and other difficulty-inducing factors, could affect the processing of the test sentences in ways which could not entirely be controlled, and they could interfere somehow with article use. For the same reason, the test was composed in such a way as to avoid false cognates (for speakers of L1 Polish) or any ambiguity.

In contrast to most tests on article use, which tend to have the classic format of a cloze test, the instrument used in this study elicited article use in a slightly different way: the text did not have gaps indicating where the participants needed to provide an article. The rationale for choosing this test design was that it is more similar to the actual use of articles than a cloze test. On a cloze test, the test taker receives a signal that an article may be missing at a specific location. In the case of those tests where the zero article is one of the options, the difference between the two formats is admittedly minor, but is still exists. In the gapped version the test taker is specifically prompted, or encouraged, to consider using an article at a specific place, and in the design employed in this study there is nothing in the test that suggests the need for an article at a specific place.

PROCEDURE

The participants took the test on a voluntary basis, in a classroom setting. They were encouraged to take the test to see how well they could use articles. The tests were coded with random three-digit combinations. Each participant was asked to write down their test number so that they would be able to retrieve their results in the future. The participants were asked to put in the missing articles in the right places. They were encouraged to follow their intuition about what sounds right. The test took around ten minutes for most participants. A time limit of 8 minutes was enforced.

8.2.3. ANALYSIS, RESULTS AND DISCUSSION

In the analysis of the data, dichotomous scores were compiled: one point was awarded for inserting a correct article, and 0 points for omitting to insert an article or for inserting an incorrect one. In the case of test items with the zero article, 1 point was given for not providing an article, and 0 points for providing an indefinite or definite article.

The mean item score was calculated for the frequent and for the rare uses for all 90 participants, as well as for each group separately. Those mean item scores are presented in Table 2. A *t*-test was performed to compare means.

	rare combinations	frequent combinations	*t*-test
All participants ($n = 90$)	0.68	0.85	$t = 9.50$; $p < 0.00001$
Group 1 (less proficient, $n = 44$)	0.53	0.75	$t = 7.44$; $p < 0.00001$
Group 2 (more proficient, $n = 46$)	0.82	0.94	$t = 6.64$; $p < 0.00001$

Table 2. Mean items scores for frequent and rare uses.

As shown by the very low *p* value yielded by the *t*-test for all 90 participants as a group, the mean for the frequent combinations is significantly higher than that for the rare ones. In other words, for the same articles and the same grammatical rule, the participants tend to be more successful when using the articles in those combinations that occur more frequently, and less likely to be correct with the less frequent combinations.

When analysed separately, both groups show higher success rates in the case of the frequent combinations than the rare ones. In both cases the difference is statistically significant. However, in the case of Group 2 (more proficient) the difference between rare and frequent combinations was smaller: a difference in means of only 0.12, compared to a difference of 0.22 in the case of the less proficient Group 1.

The fact that the difference between the rare and frequent combinations becomes smaller as the level of proficiency increases is understandable: ultimately, with very advanced language competence, there would be very little difference, as articles would be used mostly correctly in all cases for both the frequent and rare word combinations.

It should be noted that the predicted higher means for frequent items were not obtained in the case of all the pairs on the test, as shown in Table 3.

Version	Article	Target item	Mean	SD	t-value	p (t)
Frequent:	a	a friend of mine	0.80	0.4		
Rare:		an acquaintance of mine	0.48	0.5	4.75	<.0001
Frequent:	a	what a shame	0.79	0.41		
Rare:		what a remarkable player	0.81	0.39	−0.37	.71
Frequent:	a	twice a day	0.89	0.31		
Rare:		five times a semester	0.79	0.41	1.83	.04
Frequent:	the	the sooner the better	0.84	0.36		
Rare:		the smaller the pot, the more critical the problem	0.23	0.43	10.35	<.0001
Frequent:	a	a cup of tea	0.99	0.11		
Rare:		a spoonful of syrup	0.90	0.25	1.94	.02
Frequent:	the	the day I die	0.94	0.23		
Rare:		the food I brought	0.68	0.47	4.83	<.0001
Frequent:	the	help the poor	0.73	0.45		
Rare:		open to the insured	0.52	0.5	2.99	<.01
Frequent:	the	hit (someone) in the face	0.69	0.47		
Rare:		cut in the hand	0.40	0.49	4.04	<.0001
Frequent:	zero	speak English	1	0		
Rare:		learn Kurdish	0.93	0.25	2.52	.01
Frequent:	a	get a job	0.89	0.32		
Rare:		live in a luxury apartment	0.90	0.3	−0.24	.81

Version	Article	Target item	Mean	SD	*t*-value	*p* (t)
Frequent:	zero	have kids	1	0	3.34	<.01
Rare:		eat carbohydrates	0.89	0.32		
Frequent:	the	the centre of attention	0.61	0.49	0.6	.55
Rare:		the ecology of waterways	0.57	0.5		

Table 3. Compared scores for item pairs (*n* = 90).

Out of the 12 pairs of frequent-vs-rare, the differences between the means for the frequent items and their rare counterparts as shown by a *t*-test is statistically significant (at *p* < .05) for nine item pairs, and not significant for three items. The items for which the effect was not observed include: *what a shame – what a remarkable player, get a job – live in a luxury apartment*, and *the centre of attention – the ecology of waterways*. In the case of the first pair it is relatively easy to come up with a possible explanation for the observed lack of a formulaicity effect. While the phrase *what a shame* is definitely much more frequent than the rather "open-choice" word combination *what a remarkable player*, the nouns *player* and *shame* differ in the degree to which they are countable. First of all, *player* is a concrete and *shame* an abstract noun, and, as has been noted (see e.g. Amuzie & Spinner, 2013), the degree of success in article use depends on this distinction (with abstract nouns being more difficult to use correctly with articles) but also on other more nuanced distinctions which result from the degree of boundedness of a given noun. It is, therefore, possible, that the abstract and less countable character of *shame* reduced the phraseological advantage which was expected on the basis of the phrase *what a shame* being frequent. For the pair *get a job – live in a luxury apartment*, one plausible explanation is that the combination *live in a luxury apartment* was generally very easy for the test-takers; *apartment* being a clearly countable, concrete noun. The mean scores for both items were very high (0.89 and 0.9, respectively), which means that the effect of formulaicity, if any, may not have registered because of a kind of ceiling effect with the rare combination. For the last pair which did not show a difference, *the centre of attention – the ecology of waterways*, it is difficult to provide a plausible explanation of this fact.

Two item-related issues need to be addressed. One is the possible effect of adjectival pre-modification on the use of articles with nouns. In two of the test items the noun happened to be pre-modified by an adjective (*a remarkable player, a luxury apartment*), which introduced the possibility of another variable confounding the results, as there are reasons to believe that adjectival pre-modification may somehow interplay with article use by L2 English learners. This is possible in view of the fact that Trenkic (2008) found that learners from article-less language backgrounds tend to omit articles more in adjectivally pre-modified (Art+Adj+N) than in non-modified contexts (Art+N). She also offered a "syntactic misanalysis account" (Trenkic, 2007, 2008), which links the failure to use articles to the fact that articles are treated as adjectives.

In this study, the two items which included pre-modified nouns in the target items belonged to the "rare" category, thus potentially contributing to the expected lower scores for those items because of a variable that was not taken into consideration. However, for the two pairs in which the two items occur, *what a shame – what a remarkable player* and *get a job – live in a luxury apartment*, the expected effect was *not* observed. In other words, the learners were similarly successful in providing an article in both the rare and the frequent item, *despite* the fact that the rare item was additionally more likely to be more difficult due to the use of an adjective. Thus, in this study, the issue of adjectival pre-modification did not appear to play a role in article use, at least as far as one can tell on the basis of the two target items which featured adjectival pre-modification.

Another issue which needs to be addressed is the level of difficulty of some of the words. It is true that some of the "rare" items feature words of somewhat lower frequency than the "frequent" combinations. However, all the lexical items in both types of expressions were expected to be familiar to the learners, as explained in the instrument and procedure section.

An interesting finding concerns the types of wrong answers provided by the participants on the test. As stated above, in the process of compiling dichotomous scores, one point was awarded for a correctly supplied article, and 0 points were given for omitting to insert an article or for inserting an incorrect one. Out of the 512 answers for which the score was zero, an overwhelming majority (475 answers, which is almost 93%) were answers which were wrong because no article was provided. Only 37 answers were cases in which the wrong article was supplied. This indicates that, regarding article use by learners from article-less L1 backgrounds, failing to provide an article is much more common than providing an incorrect one. Of course, failing to use an article can also be seen as a case of wrong article choice, namely, the choice of the zero article. However, it is impossible to distinguish between the use of the zero article and failing to use any article (cf. Leńko-Szymańska, 2012), nor is it certain that making a distinction of this kind is feasible (see section 1.5). It should be noted that the format of the test used in this study, which did not provide a prompt to use an article in specific place in the text (as, for instance, a gapped article test would do) may have contributed to the notable underuse of articles. As far as the present analysis goes, whatever the reason for failing to use an overt article, it remains an interesting finding in its own right that the participants were much more inclined not to use an article than to use the wrong one of the two overt articles (*a(n)* or *the*).

8.3. STUDY 2

8.3.1. PARTICIPANTS

The participants were 200 undergraduate university students majoring in English studies. They were all native speakers of Polish. The students' placement in groups for their practical English classes reflected their level of proficiency, which was considered a sufficient indication of their level of knowledge for the purposes of the present study. The first group (n = 100) was at the B2 level on the CEFR (Council of Europe, 2011), whereas the second, more advanced group (n = 100) was at the C1 level. All participants were between 20 and 23 years of age, with a mean age slightly lower for Group 1.

8.3.2. INSTRUMENT AND PROCEDURE

This study investigates the use of articles by ESL learners by drawing on the concept of corpus-derived lexical bundles (see section 7.2). The main idea behind the design of the research tool was similar to that of Study 1, which was to compare learners' article use in pairs of comparable contexts which differ only with respect to the level of formulaicity. However, it adopted a different method of finding suitable test items; also, rather than have a limited number of items on each type of article use, this study focuses only on the use of the definite article.

To create an instrument that is easy to administer and does not discourage or tire test takers, efforts were taken to avoid repetitiveness while at the same time reaching a sufficient number of article occurrences, so that the target items would become "hidden" in a sufficient amount of text. The final test consisted of two parts, with isolated

sentences in one section and short texts in the other. The procedure
that led to the creation of the test is described below.

Suitable target items were selected on a data-driven basis, using the
COCA, which was selected for its relatively large size (520 million
words), and the fact that it is balanced for genre.

A) high-frequency items

A list of the most frequent 4-grams containing the definite article *the* was retrieved from the COCA. The decision was made to
study 4-grams, or 4-word bundles, as they are the most commonly
studied type of lexical bundle (see e.g. Chen & Baker, 2010). Hyland
gives the following explanation for this fact: "Three-word bundles
are extremely common, and tend not to be very interesting, while 5-
and 6-grams are comparatively rare and often subsume shorter ones.
Four-word bundles seem to be most often studied, perhaps because
they are over 10 times more frequent than five-word sequences and
offer a wider variety of structures and functions to analyse" (Hyland,
2012, p. 151).

As was said before, bundles are simply the most frequently occurring word sequences of a given length (in this case, 4-word strings).
When a list of such sequences is extracted from a corpus and ranked
according to decreasing frequency, the question arises as to the frequency beyond which the sequences lose their bundle status. Of
course, such a cut-off point must be arbitrary, as we are dealing with
not a dichotomy, but a continuum. However, for practical purposes
such a distinction is made, and some kind of consensus exists, as
most studies put that cut-off point between the frequencies 10 and

40 times per million words, depending on the purpose of the study. Biber and colleagues (e.g. Biber et al., 1999; Conrad & Biber, 2004) set the frequency minimum for 4-word sequences to be considered bundles at ten times per million words. This limit was applied in the present study, yielding a list of 42 bundles containing the definite article. Of those 42 bundles, only the ten most frequent are shown in Table 4, for the sake of brevity, but they are very representative of the rest, as the entire group of 42 bundles shares many similarities. When we apply the classification offered by Biber and his colleagues (1999) to the 42 bundles with *the*, it turns out that a vast majority belong to the category of "prepositional phrase expressions" (such as *at the end of, in the middle of, for a couple of*). Most of the remaining 4-grams belong to the type classified as "noun phrase expressions," which consist of the beginning of a noun phrase, very often including *of*, or other noun phrases and noun phrase fragments. Examples include *the end of the, the rest of the, the other side of the, the one with the, the last time I* (Biber et al., 1999, p. 1012).

In order to classify the bundles on the list in notional terms, they were compared with the taxonomy offered by Erman and Warren (2000), according to which they fall mostly into the category "period or point in time" and "places and positions." This is consistent with the observation made by Biber and colleagues that frequent noun phrase bundles usually identify a physical location, while prepositional phrase expressions are used primarily as time or place adverbials, such as *I get paid at the end of the week* (Biber et al., 1999, p. 1013). An exception to this trend is the bundle on the other hand, which is classified by Erman and Warren as grammatical, that is, "intralinguistic text-forming" rather than a unit with "extralinguistic reference" (Erman & Warren, 2000, p. 41).

1.	in	**the**	united	states	69.28
2.	**the**	end	of	the	59.17
3.	at	**the**	same	time	55.20
4.	at	**the**	end	of	47.82
5.	**the**	rest	of	the	45.40
6.	for	**the**	first	time	45.37
7.	one	of	**the**	most	38.80
8.	on	**the**	other	hand	36.69
9.	of	**the**	united	states	34.53
10.	in	**the**	middle	of	34.44

Table 4. The top ten most frequent 4-grams containing the definite article, extracted from the COCA.

For the purpose of this study, the decision was made to retain the bundles belonging to the category of prepositional phrase expressions for developing the research tool, for the following reasons:

1. Any 4-gram may happen to contain up to two articles, and the article(s) can occur in any of the four slots, but not adjacent ones (unless the four-word sequence comes from a transcript of speech and includes an instance of repetition or self-correction). Prepositional phrase bundles all feature an article in the second slot of the 4-gram. The other large group among the frequent bundles, noun phrase expressions (such as the end of the, the back of the), usually feature articles in the initial or final position, or both. When the article occurs in the initial or final position, the 4-gram only captures its syntagmatic environment on one side. Since the study aims at exploring the role of some kind of a phraseological "binding" in the use of articles, the article must not be on the edge of the 4-gram, because we wish to consider its syntagmatic environment on both sides. Obviously, articles which are captured in the final slot of a bundle are in a syntactic and semantic relationship

with the rest of the noun phrase which is not included, as in e.g. *the bundle is one of the*.

2. The prepositional phrase bundles were the most numerous among the frequent bundles (above 10 per million). Therefore, in order to eliminate a potential variable that would affect a minority of the items, it was thought better to focus on one type of bundle for designing the research instrument.

3. This decision also provided a solution to the usual problem that researchers working with lexical bundles have to deal with: the need to eliminate or conflate overlapping bundles (see e.g. Hyland, 2012, for an explanation). Such overlapping bundles can be seen, for example, in Table 4: *the end of the* and *at the end of*.

4. Prepositional phrase bundles are the ones which structurally correspond to traditionally identified bundles or prefabs (e.g. Erman & Warren, 2000), such as *in the context of, at the beginning of*, etc.

Additionally, several other items were eliminated, which are listed below.
- Two items which were idiomatic in character, in the sense of having a non-compositional meaning: *on the other hand* or *in the face of.* In those two cases, there is significant opacity of meaning, which could introduce an additional variable. In ESL instruction, such items are likely to be taught as separate, non-compositional chunks, with the meaning assigned to the whole chunk.
- A somewhat similar case was represented by *in the midst of,* which contains a word which is rare and dated if used outside of this specific word combination. For that reason, it was also removed.

Another important issue was that of the extent to which the target items would constitute obligatory occasions for the use of the definite article. Here, the situation is further complicated by the specific way in which articles are used in English. In contrast to many other morphemes, the use of articles in English is characterized by a fair amount of optionality. This means that even for contexts where the article is normally required, it may be omitted in certain situations, registers, or contexts, for example, to indicate a shorthand style caused by the speaker's haste, or in humorous uses of language. In some text types it is customary to leave out articles (for example, in culinary recipes), or in some elements of certain texts, for example newspaper headlines. There may also be other special uses, as illustrated below, such as the names of court cases. Below, there are some examples of the same word combinations which occur in our frequent bundles (*in the middle of, at the same time, in the United States*), but without the article, as found in the COCA:

> *Place mixture into muffin tins sprayed with cooking spray; bake in middle of oven for 30 minutes.*
> *At same time, roast pork until instant-read thermometer inserted in center reaches 145°F.*
> *For example, in United States v. Wilson, the defendant was charged and convicted...*

This is not the only reason, however, why article-less versions of the frequent bundles (for example, *for the first time, in the Middle East, in the United States*) may be found in the corpus. The may happen to be part of a sequence which pre-modifies a noun, as in:

> *A guide for first time researchers in education and social science...*
> *...a senior lecturer in Middle East politics at the University of Exeter...*
> *...a symphonic band like those found in United States high schools...*

However, for most of the lexical bundles, there was a striking disparity between the number of the occurrences of the lexical bundle, and its version without the article. For example, the bundle *at the same time* appears almost 29,000 times in the corpus, whereas *at same time* appears only 29 times, so the former is a thousand times more frequent. For other bundles the proportions were similar. There were only two exceptions: *in the case of* and *of the things that*. These two bundles are frequent, of course, but their article-less versions are also frequent: *in case of* appears 1478 times, and *of things that* 3484 times. Such a high number of occurrences of the article-less version of the two bundles casts doubt on the suitability of these two items for the present test. However, this conclusion needed to be further verified, because of aforementioned issues with looking up article use in a corpus, and also because the bundles had to be placed in sentence contexts for the test, which would affect whether the article would be needed or not. The sentences containing the high-frequency bundles were thus piloted on a group of native speakers ($n = 15$). A unanimous decision to put an article in a specific place was taken to mean that the place is an obligatory occasion for the use of the definite article. Indeed, the native speakers' judgments confirmed that the two items (*in the case of*, and *of the things that*) had to be eliminated, as there was variability in the use of articles in those two cases.

B) low-frequency items

For each of the 15 frequent 4-grams that remained after the elimination process described above, a corresponding low-frequency sequence was selected. The 15 bundles fall into two types, syntactically speaking. The two types are described below, with the pedagogical rules that are relevant to the use of article they represent.

I) Preposition + definite article + adjective + noun
  a) Plural geographical names are one of the sub-classes of proper nouns which are used with the definite article, for example, the Shetlands (e.g. Quirk & Greenbaum, 1973, p. 80 section 4.30); this rule is indicated in Table 5 as PL GEO NAME.
  b) A definite article is needed because of adjectival pre-modification, as in this is the main bedroom (Sinclair, 1990, p. 46); this rule is indicated in Table 5 as DEF-MOD.

II) Preposition + definite article + noun + preposition
  A definite article is needed because of postmodification by an of-phrase ("postmodification by an of-phrase usually requires the definite article with a head noun, which thus has limited generic (partitive) reference" (Quirk & Greenbaum, 1973, p. 71, section 4.19). This rule is indicated in Table 5 as OF-PHRASE.

  For both bundles of type I) and type II), the following procedure was applied when searching for suitable low-frequency equivalents. Strings analogous to the frequent ones were found in the corpus, and one was selected that had the lowest possible frequency, while also meeting other criteria. Suitable phrases had to be semantically compositional and represent instances of article use which are regular in the grammatical sense. Care was taken not to introduce additional variables: nouns were replaced with nouns which had a comparable level of concreteness, the same number, and when possible, pertaining to the same semantic field. The same "rule" was supposed to be represented by the high-frequency and the low-frequency item. This approached resulted in the following replacements, listed by type of bundle:

  • For type Ia: the adjective and the noun in a geographical name were replaced by another name with the same make-up: *the United States – the Kuril Islands.*
  • For type Ib: The adjective and the noun were replaced: for example, *for the first time – for the last lap.*

- For type II: The noun was replaced: e.g. *at the top of* – *at the underside of.*

The final pairs (lexical bundle – corresponding low frequency sequence) are listed in Table 5.

	high-frequency sequences (bundles)	freq per million	low-frequency sequence	freq per million	pedagogical rule
1.	*in the United States*	69.278	*in the Kuril Islands*	0.002	DEF-MOD / PL GEO NAME
2.	*at the same time*	55.196	*at the right level*	0.029	DEF-MOD
3.	*at the end of*	47.819	*at the closure of*	0.010	OF-PHRASE
4.	*for the first time*	45.373	*for the last lap*	0.006	DEF-MOD
5.	*in the middle of*	34.436	*in the nexus of*	0.017	OF-PHRASE
6.	*on the other side*	15.380	*on the far edge*	0.031	DEF-MOD
7.	*on the basis of*	13.988	*on the merit of*	0.017	OF-PHRASE
8.	*in the form of*	13.590	*in the phrasing of*	0.015	OF-PHRASE
9.	*for the rest of*	12.821	*for the width of*	0.023	OF-PHRASE
10.	*at the top of*	12.706	*at the underside of*	0.059	OF-PHRASE
11.	*in the middle east*	11.404	*in the distant north*	0.002	DEF-MOD
12.	*on the part of*	11.244	*on the factor of*	0.008	OF-PHRASE
13.	*at the time of*	10.638	*at the period of*	0.008	OF-PHRASE
14.	*at the beginning of*	10.085	*at the dawning of*	0.021	OF-PHRASE
15.	*in the context of*	10.046	*in the chance of*	0.015	OF-PHRASE

Table 5. The high-frequency and low-frequency pairs.

THE CREATION OF SENTENCES AND TEXTS

Like in the case of the frequent items, a sentence context was provided for the rare items. Some of the sentences containing the target items were combined into paragraphs, to avoid the monotony
of too many single sentences. The final shape of the test was 16 single sentences and two paragraphs. Naturally, the test included more
instances of article use (both definite and indefinite) than just the
articles located in the target items (all definite). In the next step, all
the articles were removed from the text and the place where they
were missing was not indicated. The task of the test-taker was to
supply the missing articles.

The entire test was piloted again on a group of native speakers
of English (n = 15) and this time also on learners of English, primarily to ensure that the removal of articles did not create ambiguous or incomprehensible sentences. A few problematic sentences
were modified with the target items remaining intact. Some of the
native speaker judges on whom the final test was piloted (who were
asked to supply articles, but they were not given an explanation as
to the purpose of the test) commented on the apparent strangeness of some of the low-frequency items, saying that they would
recommend replacing them with a "more idiomatic" expression,
or a phrase which is stylistically more felicitous. This was taken
as confirmation of the suitability of those particular sequences for
the purposes of this study, and this reaction was understandable,
given that sequences with very low frequencies convey a meaning
which is usually expressed by a more familiar phrase. Apart from
several such comments, the test was described by the participants
in the pilot study as easy and quick to complete. The final test can
be found in Appendix 1.

PROCEDURE

The participants took the test on a voluntary basis, in a classroom setting. They were encouraged to take the test to see how well they could
use articles. The tests were coded with random three-digit combinations. Each participant was asked to write down their test number so
that they would be able to retrieve their results in the future. The participants were asked to put in the missing articles in the right places
and were encouraged to follow their intuition about what sounds
right. A time limit of 15 minutes was enforced, but the test took only
around ten minutes for most participants.

8.3.3. RESULTS AND DISCUSSION

The data were compiled in the form of dichotomous scores, with
a score of 1 indicating the use of the definite article in the right
place in the target item, and a score of 0 indicating the absence of
the article or the insertion of an indefinite article. Given the nature
of the test, there were no missing data, and a data matrix of 6,000
scores (items X participants) was analysed. Mean scores for all the
participants and for the two categories of items – for frequent and
rare uses – are presented in Table 6. A t-test was performed for each
comparison, showing in each case that the scores obtained for frequent bundles are significantly higher than those for low-frequency
bundles.

	frequent sequences (bundles)	low-frequency sequences	t-test: t value
All participants ($n = 200$)	0.73	0.46	-22.21^{***}
Group 1 (less proficient, level B2, $n = 100$)	0.63	0.32	-16.14^{***}
Group 2 (more proficient, level C1, $n = 100$)	0.83	0.59	-11.96^{***}

$^{***} = p < 0.001$

Table 6. Mean items scores for frequent and rare uses.

For all the participants taken together, the mean score for the articles in the frequent bundles is 0.73, while the score for the use of articles in the rare combinations of words is 0.43. When the groups are analysed separately, a similar pattern can be observed in each case, with the success rate being higher for bundles than for rare word combinations. However, the gap between the scores for the frequent and the rare category is larger in the case of the less proficient group. In fact, for the less proficient learners, the score on frequent bundles was twice as high as that on the rare ones.

Table 7 presents the mean item scores for individual test items. As can be seen, while there is a significant difference in the means for both categories, this does not mean that all frequent items were characterised by more successful article use than all the rare items. Most notably, the frequent bundles *at the end of*, *on the part of*, and *in the form of* were supplied with the correct article less often than other frequent bundles. By far the greatest success at providing the correct article was witnessed in the case of the bundle *for the rest of*. Among the rare items, *for the last lap* scored very high for a rare word combination, with the average score of 0.68. One possible explanation of the high rate of success of this item is that the combination *for the last lap*, rare as a 4-gram, contains a frequent 3-gram, *for the last*, with the article enclosed in the middle position.

	frequent sequences (bundles)				low-frequency sequences		
		Group 1	Group 2	mean		Group 1	Group 2	mean
1.	in the united states	0.82	0.89	0.86	in the kuril islands	0.45	0.53	0.49
2.	at the same time	0.66	0.86	0.76	at the right level	0.53	0.68	0.61
3.	at the end of	0.44	0.68	0.56	at the closure of	0.19	0.43	0.31
4.	for the first time	0.76	0.91	0.84	for the last lap	0.50	0.85	0.68
5.	in the middle of	0.82	0.95	0.89	in the nexus of	0.35	0.60	0.48
6.	on the other side	0.51	0.72	0.62	on the far edge	0.25	0.54	0.40
7.	on the basis of	0.48	0.87	0.68	on the merit of	0.46	0.74	0.60
8.	in the form of	0.25	0.43	0.34	in the phrasing of	0.15	0.31	0.23
9.	for the rest of	0.93	0.94	0.94	for the width of	0.36	0.82	0.59
10.	at the top of	0.85	0.91	0.88	at the backside of	0.40	0.64	0.52
11.	in the middle east	0.89	0.81	0.85	in the distant north	0.36	0.64	0.50
12.	on the part of	0.20	0.76	0.48	on the factor of	0.30	0.68	0.49
13.	at the time of	0.72	0.96	0.84	at the period of	0.25	0.61	0.43
14.	at the beginning of	0.72	0.89	0.81	at the dawning of	0.20	0.42	0.31
15.	in the context of	0.47	0.88	0.68	in the chance of	0.10	0.38	0.24

Table 7. Mean items scores for individual test items.

When the frequencies of all items were compared to the average score for each item, it was found that there is a correlation of 0.53 ($p = 0.01$) between the two. The existence of such a correlation further confirms that there seems to be a tendency for the rate of success in article use to correspond to the frequency of the bundles; this, however, cannot be stated with much confidence given the weak correlation which was obtained. The fact that this correlation is weak was to be expected, and even a lack of a correlation in this case would be entirely understandable. The research instrument in this study was constructed in such a way that there was a major difference – a difference of three or four orders of magnitude – between the frequencies of the two categories of items – the rare and the frequent ones. It was because of this major difference that one would expect any difference between article use in the rare and frequent items to show. However, given the sometimes very small difference in the frequency of occurrence found within each of the two groups of items, especially for the frequent bundles, we could not realistically expect the same within-group differences in the degree of success in article use. For example, if the combination *on the merit of* had a frequency of 0.017, and *in the phrasing of* had a frequency of 0.015, it would be unrealistic to expect the rate of success in providing the correct article among the participants to mirror this difference in frequency. For this to happen, not only would the phraseological effect postulated here have to be very strong, there would have to be no other factors affecting the learners' performance on the test, and – most importantly – the items' frequencies in the corpus used in test construction would have to be identical to the frequencies of those items in the input the learners had been exposed to. This brings us to a certain general limitation to all studies which compare learners' performance against corpus data, namely, that the frequencies in the corpus never match those in the language input of any individual person. This limitation is widely acknowledged. In the words of Michael Hoey, "the personal 'corpus' that provides a language user with their lexical primings is by definition irretrievable, unstudiable and unique" (Hoey, 2005, p. 14). Therefore, all studies which use corpus data assume that the corpus provides information on which words are "likely to be representative of the types of input speakers are likely to have encountered" (Durrant & Doherty, 2010, p. 127).

The difference between the less proficient and the more proficient group suggests that the less advanced learners rely more on the phraseological "help" in article use which they get in the case of word combinations which may to some extent be remembered in their entirety, whereas they are less successful in applying the rules of article use in new contexts. This latter observation is entirely to be expected, since the success in using any language feature should normally grow with the level of advancement. Also, when we consider that if fully proficient, native-like users of English would provide all the correct articles for all the obligatory occasions, their score on a test like the one used in this study would be 100% for both the rare and the frequent cases. Therefore, at the ideal fully proficient level, one would expect the scores to be identical (100%) for both categories. As the learners approach this level, we should expect the gap between the rare and the frequent uses to narrow down.

There is also one more issue which deserves some thought. This study assumes that there is some formulaicity-related effect which helps learners of English choose the correct article in regular, rule-governed contexts. However, we do not know, and we are in no position to make any speculations about, the nature of this phenomenon. We know that fully proficient speakers use articles correctly. But we do not know what processes help with this use. Maybe the same formulaicity-related effect contributes to article use in general, in all language users, while at the same time being of a different nature at different stages of learning. It is theoretically possible to display the same kind of performance through the working of different mechanisms.

The participants of this study were native speakers of Polish, a language which does not have a system of articles. It is likely that similar findings would be obtained with speakers of other article-less languages, but more studies with learners of other L1 backgrounds are needed to confirm this.

Conclusion

This book introduces and explores a phraseological perspective on the use of articles in L2 English. It argues that the correct use of articles in English by non-native speakers is aided by cognitive processes related to the formulaic character of language processing. However, the dominant view during the last century was that articles are primarily an element of the morphosyntax of English, and that the successful learning of articles consists of mastering relevant morphosyntactic rules. As a result, pedagogical grammars and teaching materials traditionally reflect the misconception that a limited set of rules will lead to using articles correctly in English, with the exception of some idiomatic or fixed uses, which have to be memorized. The first chapters of this book give an overview of how articles are conceptualized and their usage accounted for within various descriptive frameworks and theoretical approaches. This overview not only brings home the extent of the complexity of the principles that underlie the use of articles, but it also makes it clear that articles to a great extent elude description and explanation. Most importantly, "rules" turn out to be at best collections of regularities. Attempts at providing a definitive set of rules governing article use fail to account for the wide array of possible uses in written and spoken English. This means that the task facing L2 learners is indeed challenging.

After providing this broad overview of article use in English, this book presents two studies conducted on the topic of formulaicity and article use. In the first study, Polish ESL learners were consistently more successful at using articles when they appear in word combinations that are frequent, which can be interpreted as a sign of the idiom principle at work. The two main observations that emerged from Study 1 are that the "phraseological effect" is more apparent in less advanced learners of English, and that articles remain an area of difficulty even at advanced levels of English proficiency, as was previously found in research.

The results obtained in the second study also show that learners are generally more likely to use the definite article correctly if the obligatory occasion for its use occurs inside a lexical bundle than if the context for its use is a combination of words which do not frequently co-occur. The findings thus suggest that the correct use of articles by ESL learners may be facilitated by phraseological ties between words.

The data from both studies allow for the tentative conclusion that phraseological effects contribute to successful article use even in those contexts when the use of articles is consistent with the patterns of regularities normally observed in English. This in turn implies that the widespread perception of the process of learning to use articles in ESL correctly as being a process of rule application needs to be broadened to acknowledge that phraseological effects contribute to mastering the use of articles. It must be stressed that the studies presented here are explorative and are only an initial investigation of the topic. Further research is needed to explore the nature and effect of collocations on article use, and how those evolve over the course of L2 development.

Understandably, the extent of the research presented here is not sufficient to make firm recommendations concerning the teaching of articles. However, if their findings are supported by future studies, a number of teaching techniques could be recommended for introduction into ESL pedagogy which would encourage the "collocational" learning of articles. Finally, because the available literature so far has shown that learners of "articled" and article-less languages seem to fall into two distinct groups with respect to article use, it is reasonable to assume that findings on the use of articles by Polish learners of L2 English may be generalizable to other article-less languages. Research with such populations is thus warranted.

References

Acton, E. K. (2014). *Pragmatics and the social meaning of determiners* (doctoral dissertation). Stanford University.

Amuzie, G. L., & Spinner, P. (2013). Korean EFL learners' indefinite article use with four types of abstract nouns. *Applied Linguistics, 34*(4), 415–434. https://doi.org/10.1093/applin/ams065

Andersen, R. W. (1984). The one to one principle of interlanguage construction. *Language Learning, 34*(4), 77–95.

Andringa, S., & Rebuschat, P. (2015). New directions in the study of implicit and explicit learning. *Studies in Second Language Acquisition, 37*(02), 185–196. https://doi.org/10.1017/S027226311500008X

Arabski, J. (1968). A linguistic analysis of English composition errors made by Polish students. *Studia Anglica Posnaniensia, 1*, 71–89.

Arabski, J. (1990). The acquisition of articles and hierarchy of difficulty. In J. Arabski (Ed.), *Foreign language acquisition papers* (pp. 11–17). Katowice: Uniwersytet Śląski.

Arabski, J., & Wojtaszek, A. (2016). Contemporary perspectives on crosslinguistic influence. In R. Alonso Alonso (Ed.), *Crosslinguistic influence in second language acquisition* (pp. 215–224). Clevedon: Multilingual Matters.

Ariel, M. (1990). *Accessing noun-phrase antecedents.* London: Routledge.

Arnon, I., & Snider, N. (2010). More than words: Frequency effects for multi-word phrases. *Journal of Memory and Language, 62*, 67–82. https://doi.org/10.1016/j.jml.2009.09.005

Bahns, J., & Eldaw, M. (1993). Should we teach EFL students collocations? *System, 21*(1), 101–114.

Benson, M., Benson, E., & Ilson, R. (1986). *The BBI combinatory dictionary of English*. Amsterdam: John Benjamins.

Berezowski, L. (2009). *The myth of the zero article*. London, New York: Continuum.

Biber, D. (2009). A corpus-driven approach to formulaic language in English: Multi-word patterns in speech and writing. *International Journal of Corpus Linguistics, 14*(3), 275–311. https://doi.org/10.1075/ijcl.14.3.08bib

Biber, D., Johansson, S., Leech, G., Conrad, S., & Finegan, E. (1999). *Longman grammar of spoken and written English*. Harlow: Pearson.

Bickerton, D. (1981). *Roots of language*. Ann Arbor, MI: Karoma.

Bielak, J. (2011). Cognitive linguistics and foreign language pedagogy: An overview of recent trends and developments. In M. Pawlak (Ed.), *Extending the boundaries of research on second language learning and teaching* (pp. 241–262). Heidelberg: Springer.

Birner, B., & Ward, G. (1994). Uniqueness, familiarity, and the definite article in English. In *Proceedings of the Twentieth Annual Meeting of the Berkeley Linguistics Society* (pp. 93–102). Berkeley, CA: Berkeley Linguistics Society.

Bitchener, J., & Knoch, U. (2010). Raising the linguistic accuracy level of advanced L2 writers with written corrective feedback. *Journal of Second Language Writing, 19*(4), 207–217. https://doi.org/10.1016/j.jslw.2010.10.002

Bod, R., Hay, J., & Jannedy, S. (Eds.). (2003). *Probabilistic linguistics*. Cambridge, London: MIT Press.

Boers, F., & Lindstromberg, S. (2012). Experimental and intervention studies on formulaic sequences in a second language. *Annual Review of Applied Linguistics, 32*, 83–110. https://doi.org/10.1017/S0267190512000050

Bolander, M. (1989). Prefabs, patterns and rules in interaction? Formulaic speech in adult learners' L2 Swedish. In K. Hyltenstam & L. K. Obler (Eds.), *Bilingualism across the lifespan: Aspects of acquisition, maturity and loss* (pp. 73–86). Cambridge: Cambridge University Press.

Brinton, L. J., & Brinton, D. M. (2010). *The linguistic structure of modern English*. Amsterdam, Philadelphia: John Benjamins.

Brown, R. (1973). *A first language: The early stages*. Cambridge, MA: Harvard University Press.

Butler, Y. G. (2002). Second language learners' theories on the use of English articles. *Studies in Second Language Acquisition, 24*(03), 451–480. https://doi.org/10.1017/S0272263102003042

Bybee, J. (2006). From usage to grammar: The mind's response to repetition. *Language, 82*(4), 711–733.

Bybee, J. (2007). *Frequency of use and the organization of language*. Oxford: Oxford University Press.

Bybee, J., & Hopper, P. (Eds.). (2001). *Frequency and the emergence of linguistic structure*. Amsterdam: John Benjamins.

Carroll, J. (1981). Twenty-five years of research on foreign language aptitude. In K. C. Diller (Ed.), *Individual differences and universals in language learning aptitude* (pp. 83–117). Rowley, MA: Newbury House.

Carter, R., & McCarthy, M. (2006). *Cambridge grammar of English*. Cambridge: Cambridge University Press.

Chase, W. G., & Simon, H. A. (1973). Perception in chess. *Cognitive Psychology*, 4, 55–81.

Chater, N., & Manning, C. D. (2006). Probabilistic models of language processing and acquisition. *Trends in Cognitive Science, 10*(7), 335–344. https://doi.org/10.1016/j.tics.2006.05.006

Chaudron, C., & Parker, K. (1990). Discourse markedness and structural markedness: The acquisition of English noun phrases. *Studies in Second Language Acquisition, 12*, 43–64.

Chen, Y.-H., & Baker, P. (2010). Lexical bundles in L1 and L2 academic writing. *Language Learning and Technology, 14*(2), 30–49. https://doi.org/10.4304/tpls.2.3.637-641

Chrabaszcz, A., & Jiang, N. (2014). The role of the native language in the use of the English nongeneric definite article by L2 learners: A cross-linguistic comparison. *Second Language Research, 30*(3), 351–379. https://doi.org/10.1177/0267658313493432

Christophersen, P. (1939). *The articles: A study of their theory and use in English*. Copenhagen: Munksgaard.

Conklin, K., & Schmitt, N. (2012). The processing of formulaic language. *Annual Review of Applied Linguistics, 32*, 45–61. https://doi.org/10.1017/S0267190512000074

Conrad, S., & Biber, D. (2004). The frequency and use of lexical bundles in conversation and academic prose. *Lexicographica, 20*, 56–71. https://doi.org/10.1515/9783484604674.56

Council of Europe. (2011). *Common European framework of reference for language: Learning, teaching, assessment*. Council of Europe.

Cruse, D. (1986). *Lexical semantics*. Cambridge: Cambridge University Press.

Cziko, G. (1986). Testing the language bioprogram hypothesis: A review of children's acquisition of articles. *Language, 62*, 878–898.

Davies, M. (2004). BYU-BNC: Based on the British National Corpus from Oxford University Press. Retrieved from https://www.english-corpora.org/bnc/

Davies, M. (2008). The Corpus of Contemporary American English (COCA). Retrieved from https://www.english-corpora.org/coca/

Dechert, H. W. (1983). How a story is done in a second language. In C. Faerch & G. Kasper (Eds.), *Strategies in interlanguage communication* (pp. 175–195). London: Longman.

DeKeyser, R. M. (2003). Implicit and explicit learning. In C. J. Doughty & M. H. Long (Eds.), *The handbook of second language acquisition* (pp. 313–348). Malden: Blackwell.

DeKeyser, R. M. (2005). What makes learning second-language grammar difficult? A review of issues. *Language Learning, 55*(S1), 1–25.

DeKeyser, R. M. (2016). Of moving targets and chameleons: Why the concept of difficulty is so hard to pin down. *Studies in Second Language Acquisition, 38*(2), 353–363. https://doi.org/10.1017/S0272263116000024

Deprez, V., Sleeman, P., & Guella, H. (2011). Specificity effects in L2 determiner acquisition: UG or pragmatic egocentrism? In M. Pirvulescu (Ed.), *Selected proceedings of the 4th Conference on Generative Approaches to Language Acquisition North America (GALANA 2010)* (pp. 27–36). Somerville, MA: Cascadilla Proceedings Project.

Deuter, M., Greenan, J., Noble, J., & Phillips, J. (Eds.). (2002). *Oxford collocations dictionary for students of English.* Oxford: Oxford University Press.

Dienes, Z., & Perner, J. (2002). The metacognitive implications of the implicit-explicit distinction. In P. Chambres, M. Izaute, & P. J. Marescaux (Eds.), *Metacognition* (pp. 171–189). Boston, MA: Springer US. https://doi.org/10.1007/978-1-4615-1099-4_12

Dietz, G. (2002). On rule complexity: A structural approach. *EuroSLA Yearbook, 2,* 263–286.

Díez-Bedmar, M. B., & Papp, S. (2008). The use of the English article system by Chinese and Spanish learners. In G. Gilquin, S. Papp, & M. B. Díez-Bedmar (Eds.), *Linking up contrastive and learner corpus research* (pp. 147–175). Amsterdam: Rodopi.

Donnellan, K. S. (1968). Putting Humpty Dumpty together again. *Philosophical Review, 77,* 203–215.

Dörnyei, Z. (2009). *The psychology of second language learning.* Oxford: Oxford University Press.

Dörnyei, Z., & Skehan, P. (2003). Individual differences in second language learning. In C. J. Doughty & M. H. Long (Eds.), *The handbook of second language acquisition* (pp. 589 – 630). Oxford: Blackwell.

Douglas Kozłowska, C., & Dzierżanowska, H. (1988). *Selected English collocations.* Warsaw: Wydawnictwo Naukowe PWN.

Downing, A., & Locke, P. (1992). *A university course in English grammar.* Phoenix: Prentice Hall.

Durrant, P., & Doherty, A. (2010). Are high-frequency collocations psychologically real? Investigating the thesis of collocational priming. *Corpus Linguistics and Linguistic Theory, 6*(2), 125–155. https://doi.org/10.1515/cllt.2010.006

Durrant, P., & Schmitt, N. (2009). To what extent do native and non-native writers make use of collocations? *IRAL - International Review of Applied Linguistics in Language Teaching, 47*(2), 157–177. https://doi.org/10.1515/iral.2009.007

Durrant, P., & Schmitt, N. (2010). Adult learners' retention of collocations from exposure. *Second Language Research, 26*(2), 163–188. https://doi.org/10.1177/0267658309349431

Dušková, L. (1969). On sources of errors in foreign language learning. *IRAL - International Review of Applied Linguistics in Language Teaching, 7*(1), 11–36. https://doi.org/10.1515/iral.1969.7.1.11

Ekiert, M. (2004). Acquisition of the English article system by speakers of Polish in ESL and EFL Settings. *Teachers College, Columbia University Working Papers in TESOL & Applied Linguistic, 4*(1), 1–23.

Ekiert, M. (2007). The acquisition of grammatical marking of indefiniteness with the indefinite article *a* in L2 English. *Columbia University Working Papers in TESOL & Applied Linguistics, 7*(1), 1–43.

Ekiert, M., & Han, Z. (2017). L1-fraught difficulty: The case of L2 acquisition of English Articles by Slavic Speakers. In R. Alonso (Ed.), *Crosslinguistic influence in second language acquisition* (pp. 147–172). Clevedon: Multilingual Matters. https://doi.org/10.1007/978-3-319-49959-8

Ellis, N. C. (2003). Constructions, chunking, and connectionism: The emergence of second language structure. In C. J. Doughty & M. H. Long (Eds.), *The handbook of second language acquisition* (pp. 63–103). Malden, Oxford: Blackwell.

Ellis, N. C. (2005). At the interface: Dynamic interactions of explicit and implicit language knowledge. *Studies in Second Language Acquisition, 27*(2), 305–352. https://doi.org/10.1017/S027226310505014X

Ellis, N. C. (2006). Selective attention and transfer phenomena in L2 acquisition: Contingency, cue competition, salience, interference, overshadowing, blocking, and perceptual learning. *Applied Linguistics, 27*(2), 164–194. https://doi. org/10.1093/applin/amlo15

Ellis, N. C. (2015). Implicit AND explicit language learning: Their dynamic interface and complexity. In P. Rebuschat (Ed.), *Implicit and explicit learning of languages* (pp. 3–24). Amsterdam, Philadelphia: John Benjamins.

Ellis, N. C. (2016). Salience, cognition, language complexity, and complex adaptive systems. *Studies in Second Language Acquisition, 38*(2), 341–351. https:// doi.org/10.1017/S027226311600005X

Ellis, R. (2006). Current issues in the teaching of grammar: An SLA perspective. *TESOL Quarterly, 40*(1), 83–107.

Ellis, R. (2008). Investigating grammatical difficulty in second language learning: Implications for second language acquisition research and language testing. *International Journal of Applied Linguistics, 18*(1), 4–22. https://doi.org/10.1111/ j.1473-4192.2008.00184.x

Epstein, R. (2002). The definite article, accessibility, and the construction of discourse referents. *Cognitive Linguistics, 12*(4), 333–378.

Erman, B., & Warren, B. (2000). The idiom principle and the open choice principle. *Text – Interdisciplinary Journal for the Study of Discourse, 20*(1), 29–62. https://doi.org/10.1515/text.1.2000.20.1.29

Evans, V. (2007). *A glossary of cognitive linguistics.* Edinburgh: Edinburgh University Press.

Fauconnier, G. (1994). *Mental spaces: Aspects of meaning construction in natural language.* Cambridge: Cambridge University Press.

Firbas, J. (1992). *Functional sentence perspective in written and spoken communication.* Cambridge: Cambridge University Press.

Gablasova, D., Brezina, V., & McEnery, T. (2017). Collocations in corpus-based language learning research: Identifying, comparing, and interpreting the evidence. *Language Learning, 67,* 155–179. https://doi.org/10.1111/lang.12225

Gass, S. M., & Selinker, L. (2008). *Second language acquisition: An introductory course* (3rd edition). New York, London: Routledge.

Gass, S. M., Spinner, P., & Behney, J. (Eds.). (2018). *Salience in second language acquisition.* New York: Routledge.

Gillian, E. J. (2017). *Gil's Article Maker. An interactive tool for teaching English article use to Polish gimnazjum students: Development and evaluation* (doctoral dissertation). Wydział Anglistyki Uniwersytetu Adama Mickiewicza.

Głaz, A. (2012). *Extended vantage theory in linguistic application: The case of the English articles*. Lublin: Wydawnictwo Uniwersytetu Marii Curie-Skłodowskiej.

Gobet, F., Lane, P. C. R., Croker, S., Cheng, P. C. H., Jones, G., Oliver, I., & Pine, J. M. (2001). Chunking mechanisms in human learning. *Trends in Cognitive Sciences, 5*(6), 236–243. https://doi.org/10.1016/S1364-6613(00)01662-4

Godfroid, A. (2016). The effects of implicit instruction on implicit and explicit knowledge development. *Studies in Second Language Acquisition, 38*(2), 177–215. https://doi.org/10.1017/S0272263115000388

Goldberg, A. E. (2006). *Constructions at work: The nature of generalization in language*. Oxford: Oxford University Press.

Goldschneider, J. M., & DeKeyser, R. M. (2005). Explaining the "natural order of L2 morpheme acquisition" in English: A meta-analysis of multiple determinants. *Language Learning, 55*(1), 27–77.

Gozdawa-Gołębiowski, R. (2003). *Interlanguage formation: A study of the triggering mechanisms*. Warsaw: Instytut Anglistyki UW.

Granfeldt, J. (2000). The acquisition of the Determiner Phrase in bilingual and second-language French. *Bilingualism: Language and Cognition, 3*(3), 263–280.

Granger, S. (1998). *Learner English on computer*. London: Routledge.

Granger, S., & Meunier, F. (2008). The many faces of phraseology. In S. Granger & F. Meunier (Eds.), *Phraseology: An interdisciplinary perspective* (pp. xix–xxviii). Amsterdam, Philadelphia: John Benjamins.

Greenbaum, S. (1991). *An introduction to English Grammar*. Harlow: Longman.

Grice, P. (1975). Logic and conversation. In P. Cole & J. L. Morgan (Eds.), *Syntax and semantics* (Vol. 3, pp. 41–58). New York: Academic Press.

Gries, S. T., & Ellis, N. C. (2015). Statistical measures for usage-based linguistics. *Language Learning, 65*(S1), 228–255. https://doi.org/10.1111/lang.12119

Hakuta, K. (1976). A case study of a Japanese child learning English. *Language Learning, 26*(2), 321–351. https://doi.org/10.1111/j.1467-1770.1976.tb00280.x

Halliday, M. A. K. (1961). Categories of the theory of grammar. *WORD, 17*(2), 241–292. https://doi.org/10.1080/00437956.1961.11659756

Halliday, M. A. K., & Hasan, R. (1976). *Cohesion in English*. London: Longman.

Hallin, A. E., & Van Lancker Sidtis, D. (2017). A closer look at formulaic language: Prosodic characteristics of Swedish proverbs. *Applied Linguistics, 38*(1), 68–89. https://doi.org/10.1093/applin/amu078

Hamrick, P. (2014). A role for chunk formation in statistical learning of second language syntax. *Language Learning, 64*(2), 247–278. https://doi.org/10.1111/lang.12049

Hawkins, J. A. (1978). *Definiteness and indefiniteness: A study in reference and grammaticality prediction*. London: Croom Helm.

Hawkins, J. A. (1984). A note on referent identifiability and co-presence. *Journal of Pragmatics, 8*(5–6), 649–659.

Hawkins, J. A. (1991). On (in)definite articles: Implicatures and (un)grammaticality prediction. *Journal of Linguistics, 27*(2), 405–442.

Hawkins, R. (2001). *Second language syntax: A generative introduction*. Oxford: Blackwell.

Hawkins, R., Al-Eid, S., Almahboob, I., Athanasopoulos, P., Chaengchenkit, R., Hu, J., ... Velasco-Zarate, K. (2006). Accounting for English article interpretation by L2 speakers. *EUROSLA Yearbook, 6*, 7–25.

Hewson, J. (1964). *Article and noun in English: An essay in psychomechanical analysis*. Ste-Foy, Québec: Université Laval.

Hiki, M. (1991). *A study of learners' judgment on noun countability* (doctoral dissertation). Indiana University.

Hinenoya, K., & Lyster, R. (2015). Identifiability and accessibility in learning definite article usages: A quasi-experimental study with Japanese learners of English. *Language Teaching Research, 19*(4), 397–415. https://doi.org/10.1177/1362168814541742

Hoey, M. (2005). *Lexical priming: A new theory of words and language*. London: Routledge.

Holme, R. (2007). *Cognitive linguistics and language teaching*. New York: Palgrave Macmillan.

Holmes, J. (1988). Doubt and certainty in ESL textbooks. *Applied Linguistics, 9*(1), 21–44.

Housen, A., & Simoens, H. (2016). Cognitive perspectives on difficulty and complexity in L2 acquisition. *Studies in Second Language Acquisition, 38*(2), 163–175. https://doi.org/10.1017/S0272263116000176

Howarth, P. A. (1996). *Phraseology in English academic writing: Some implications for language learning and dictionary making*. Berlin: De Gruyter.

Hsu, J. T. (2008). Role of the multiword lexical units in current EFL ESL textbooks. *US-China Foreign Language, 6*(7), 27–39.

Hua, D., & Lee, T. H.-t. (2005). Chinese ESL learners' understanding of the English count-mass distinction. In R. Dekydtspotter, A. Sprouse, & A. Liljestrand (Eds.), *Proceedings of the 7th Generative Approaches to Second Language Acquisition Conference* (pp. 139–149). Somerville, MA: Cascadilla Proceedings Project.

Huddleston, R., & Pullum, G. K. (2002). *The Cambridge grammar of the English language*. Cambridge, New York, Melbourne: Cambridge University Press.

Hudson, R. (2004). Are determiners heads? *Functions of Language, 11*(1), 7–42.

Huebner, T. (1983). *A longitudinal analysis of the acquisition of English*. Ann Arbor, MI: Karoma.

Huebner, T. (1985). System and variability in interlanguage syntax. *Language Learning, 35*(2), 141–163.

Hulstijn, J. H. (2005). Theoretical and empirical issues in the study of implicit and explicit second-language learning. *Studies in Second Language Acquisition, 27*, 129–140.

Hyland, K. (2012). Bundles in academic discourse. *Annual Review of Applied Linguistics, 32*, 150–169. https://doi.org/10.1017/S0267190512000037

Ionin, T., Ko, H., & Wexler, K. (2004). Article semantics in L2-acquisition: the role of specificity. *Language Acquisition, 12*, 3–69.

Ionin, T., Zubizarreta, M. L., & Maldonado, S. B. (2008). Sources of linguistic knowledge in the second language acquisition of English articles. *Lingua, 118*(4), 554–576. https://doi.org/10.1016/j.lingua.2006.11.012

Jarvis, S. (2002). Topic continuity in L2 English article use. *Studies in Second Language Acquisition, 24*(3), 387–418. https://doi.org/10.1017/S0272263102003029

Jiang, N., & Nekrasova, T. M. (2007). The processing of formulaic sequences by second language speakers. *The Modern Language Journal, 91*(3), 433–445. https://doi.org/10.1111/j.1540-4781.2007.00589.x

Jones, S., & Sinclair, J. M. (1974). English lexical collocations. *Cahiers de Lexicologie, 24*, 15–61.

Kaltenbacher, M. (2001). *Universal Grammar and parameter resetting in second language acquisition*. Frankfurt: Peter Lang.

Kałuża, H. (1963). Teaching the English articles to speakers of Slavic. *Language Learning, 13*(2), 113–124. https://doi.org/10.1111/j.1467-1770.1963.tb01290.x

Kambarov, Z. (2008). *The concept of definiteness and its application to automated reference resolution*. New York: Peter Lang.

Kharma, N. (1981). Analysis of the errors committed by Arab university students in the use of the English definite/indefinite articles. *International Review of Applied Linguistics, 19*, 331–345.

Krashen, S. D. (1985). *The Input Hypothesis*. London and New York: Longman.

Kreidler, C. W. (1998). *Introducing English semantics*. London: Routledge.

Król, A. (2005). *Applied cognitive linguistics in teaching English articles to Polish learners*. Essen: University of Duisburg.

Król-Markefka, A. (2008). Some theoretical considerations on the use of contrastive data in teaching English articles to Polish learners. *Studia Linguistica Universitatis Iagellonicae Cracoviensis, 125*, 103–112.

Król-Markefka, A. (2010). *Metalinguistic knowledge and the accurate use of English articles: Effects of applying cognitive grammar in second language teaching* (doctoral dissertation). Jagiellonian University.

Król-Markefka, A. (2012). Pedagogical rules for the use of English articles: An evaluation and suggestions for improvement. *Studia Linguistica Universitatis Iagellonicae Cracoviensis, 129*, 98–115. https://doi.org/10.4467/2083462 4SL.12.007.0596

Kuiper, K. (2004). Formulaic performance in conventionalized varieties of speech. In N. Schmitt (Ed.), *Formulaic sequences: acquisition, processing and use* (pp. 37–54). Amsterdam: John Benjamins.

Langacker, R. W. (1987). *Foundations of Cognitive Grammar*. Stanford: Stanford University Press.

Langacker, R. W. (2000). *A dynamic usage-based model*. Stanford: CSLI.

Larsen-Freeman, D. (1975). The acquisition of grammatical morphemes by adult ESL students. *Tesol Quarterly, 9*(4), 409–419. https://doi.org/10.2307/3585625

Laufer, B. (1997). What's in a word that makes it hard or easy? Intralexical factors affecting the difficulty of vocabulary acquisition. In N. Schmitt & M. McCarthy (Eds.), *Vocabulary: Description, acquisition and pedagogy* (pp. 140–155). Cambridge: Cambridge University Press.

Laufer, B., & Waldman, T. (2011). Verb-noun collocations in second language writing: A corpus analysis of learners' English. *Language Learning, 61*(2), 647–672. https://doi.org/10.1111/j.1467-9922.2010.00621.x

Leńko-Szymańska, A. (2012). The role of conventionalized language in the acquisition and use of articles by Polish EFL learners. In Y. Tono, Y. Kawaguchi, & M. Minegishi (Eds.), *Developmental and crosslinguistic perspectives in learner corpus research* (pp. 83–104). Amsterdam, Philadelphia: John Benjamins.

Leow, R. P. (2015). *Explicit learning in the L2 classroom: A student-centered approach*. New York: Routledge.

Leśniewska, J. (2003). *The collocational aspects of advanced EFL learners' lexical competence* (doctoral dissertation). Jagiellonian University.

Leśniewska, J. (2016). The use of articles in L2 English: A phraseological perspective. *Studies in Second Language Learning and Teaching, 6*(2), 203–224.
https://doi.org/10.14746/ssllt.2016.6.2.2

Leśniewska, J. (2017). New perspectives on the use of articles in L2 English. In
L. Torres-Zúñiga & T. H. Schmidt (Eds.), *New methodological approaches
to foreign language teaching* (pp. 67–82). Newcastle upon Tyne: Cambridge
Scholars Publishing.

Li, H., & Yang, L. (2010). An investigation of English articles' acquisition by Chinese learners of English. *Chinese Journal of Applied Linguistics, 33*(3), 15–31.

Lightbown, P. M., & Spada, N. (2006). *How languages are learned* (5th edition).
Oxford: Oxford University Press.

Lin, P. M. S. (2012). Sound evidence: The missing piece of the jigsaw in formulaic
language research. *Applied Linguistics, 33*(3), 342–347. https://doi.org/10.1093/
applin/ams017

Lin, P. M. S., & Adolphs, S. (2009). Sound evidence: Phraseological units in spoken
corpora. In A. Barfield & H. Gyllstad (Eds.), *Researching collocations in another
language: Multiple interpretations* (pp. 34–48). London: Palgrave Macmillan.

Littlemore, J. (2001). *Applying cognitive linguistics to second language learning
and teaching*. New York: Palgrave Macmillan.

Liu, D., & Gleason, J. (2002). Acquisition of the article *the* by nonnative speakers
of English: An analysis of four nongeneric uses. *Studies in Second Language
Acquisition, 24*, 1–26.

Low, R. M. H. (2005). *The phenomenon of the word* the *in English: Discourse
functions and distribution patterns* (doctoral dissertation). State University
of New York.

Lyons, C. (1999). *Definiteness*. Cambridge: Cambridge University Press.

Lyons, J. (1977). *Semantics*. Cambridge, London, New York, Melbourne: Cambridge University Press.

Lyons, J. (1995). *Linguistic semantics*. Cambridge: Cambridge University Press.

MacLaury, R. E. (1995). Vantage theory. In R. E. MacLaury & J. R. Taylor (Eds.),
Language and the cognitive construal of the world (pp. 231–276). Berlin and
New York: Mouton de Gruyter.

MacWhinney, B. (2006). Emergentism – use often and with care. *Applied Linguistics, 27*(4), 729–740. https://doi.org/10.1093/applin/aml035

Maratsos, M. (1976). *The use of definite and indefinite reference in young children:
An experimental study of semantic acquisition*. Cambridge: Cambridge University Press.

Master, P. (1997). The English article system: Acquisition, function, and pedagogy. *System*, *25*(2), 215–232. https://doi.org/10.1016/S0346-251X(97)00010-9

Master, P. (2002). Information structure and English article pedagogy. *System*, *30*(3), 331–348. https://doi.org/10.1016/S0346-251X(02)00018-0

Meunier, F. (2012). Formulaic language and language teaching. *Annual Review of Applied Linguistics*, *32*, 111–129. https://doi.org/10.1017/S0267190512000128

Miller, J. (2005). Most of ESL students have trouble with the articles. *International Education Journal*, *5*(5), 80–88. https://doi.org/10.1016/S1351-4180(14)70140-0

Mitchell, B., & Robinson, F. C. (1992). *A guide to Old English* (5th edition). Oxford: Blackwell.

Mueller, C. M. (2011). English learners' knowledge of prepositions: Collocational knowledge or knowledge based on meaning? *System*, *39*(4), 480–490. https://doi.org/10.1016/j.system.2011.10.012

Muñoz, C., & Singleton, D. (2011). A critical review of age-related research on L2 ultimate attainment. *Language Teaching*, *44*(1), 1–35. https://doi.org/10.1017/S0261444810000327

Myles, F., & Cordier, C. (2016). Formulaic sequence (FS) cannot be an umbrella term in SLA. *Studies in Second Language Acquisition*, *39*(1), 1–26. https://doi.org/10.1017/S027226311600036X

Myles, F., Hooper, J., & Mitchell, R. (1998). Rote or rule? Exploring the role of formulaic language in classroom foreign language learning. *Language Learning*, *48*(3), 323–364.

Nation, I. S. P. (2001). *Learning vocabulary in another language*. Cambridge: Cambridge University Press.

Nattinger, J., & DeCarrico, J. (1992). *Lexical phrases and language teaching*. Oxford: Oxford University Press.

Neale, S. (1990). *Descriptions*. Cambridge, MA: MIT Press.

Nekrasova, T. M. (2009). English L1 and L2 speakers' knowledge of lexical bundles. *Language Learning*, *59*(3), 647–686. https://doi.org/10.1111/j.1467-9922.2009.00520.x

Nesselhauf, N. (2003). The use of collocations by advanced learners of English and some implications for teaching. *Applied Linguistics*, *24*(2), 223–242.

Ogawa, M. (2008). The acquisition of English articles by advanced EFL Japanese learners : Analysis based on noun types. *Journal of Language and Culture, Language and Information*, *3*, 133–151.

Palmer, F. R. (1981). *Semantics* (2nd edition). Cambridge, New York, Melbourne: Cambridge University Press.

Paradowski, M. B. (2006). Uczyć, aby nauczyć – rola języka ojczystego w gramatyce pedagogicznej i implikacje dla dydaktyki języków obcych. In J. Krieger-Knieja & U. Paprocka-Piotrowska (Eds.), *Komunikacja językowa w społeczeństwie informacyjnym – nowe wyzwania dla dydaktyki języków obcych* (pp. 125–144). Lublin: Towarzystwo Naukowe KUL.

Paradowski, M. B. (2008). Introducing language interface in pedagogical grammar. In D. Gabryś-Barker (Ed.), *Morphosyntactic issues in second language acquisition* (pp. 225–252). Clevedon: Multilingual Matters.

Park, K. (1996). *The article acquisition in English as a foreign language.* Retrieved from https://files.eric.ed.gov/fulltext/ED397647.pdf

Parrish, B. (1987). A new look at methodologies in the study of article acquisition for learners of ESL. *Language Learning, 37*(3), 361–383.

Parrott, M. (2000). *Grammar for English language teachers.* Cambridge: Cambridge University Press.

Pawlak, M. (2006). *The place of form-focused instruction in the foreign language classroom.* Kalisz, Poznań: Uniwersytet Adama Mickiewicza.

Pawley, A., & Syder, F. H. (1983). Two puzzles for linguistic theory: Nativelike selection and nativelike fluency. In J. C. Richards & R. W. Schmidt (Eds.), *Language and communication* (pp. 191 – 226). London: Longman.

Peters, A. M. (1977). Language learning strategies: Does the whole equal the sum of the parts? *Language, 53,* 560–73.

Peters, A. M. (1983). *The units of language acquisition.* Cambridge: Cambridge University Press.

Pichette, F., & Leśniewska, J. (2018). Percentage of L1-based errors in ESL: An update on Ellis (1985). *International Journal of Language Studies, 12*(2), 1–16.

Quirk, R., & Greenbaum, S. (1973). *A concise grammar of contemporary English.* New York: Harcourt Brace Jovanovich.

Quirk, R., Greenbaum, S., Leech, G., & Svartvik, J. (1985). *A comprehensive grammar of the English language.* London: Longman.

Raupach, M. (1984). Formulae in second language speech production. In H. Dechert, D. Möhle, & M. Raupach (Eds.), *Second language productions* (pp. 114–137). Tübingen: Gunter Narr.

Rebuschat, P., & Williams, J. N. (2012). *Statistical learning and language acquisition.* Berlin: Mouton de Gruyter.

Ringbom, H. (1985). The influence of Swedish on the English of Finnish learners. In *Foreign language learning and bilingualism* (pp. 39–71). Abo: Abo Akademi.

Roehr-Brackin, K. (2015). Explicit knowledge about language in L2 learning: A usage-based perspective. In P. Rebuschat (Ed.), *Implicit and explicit learning of languages* (pp. 117–138). Amsterdam, Philadelphia: John Benjamins.

Roehr, K., & Gánem-Gutiérrez, G. A. (2009). Metalinguistic knowledge: A stepping stone towards L2 proficiency? In A. Benati (Ed.), *Issues in second language proficiency* (pp. 79–94). London: Continuum.

Romberg, A. R., & Saffran, J. R. (2010). Statistical learning and language acquisition. *Wiley Interdisciplinary Reviews: Cognitive Science, 1*(6), 906–914. https://doi.org/10.1002/wcs.78

Rudzka, B., Channell, J., Putseys, Y., & Ostyn, P. (1981). *The words you need.* London: Macmillan.

Rudzka, B., Channell, J., Putseys, Y., & Ostyn, P. (1985). *More words you need.* London: Macmillan.

Rumelhart, D., & McClelland, J. (Eds.). (1986). *Parallel distributed processing: Explorations in the microstructure of cognition.* Cambridge: MIT Press.

Russel, B. (1905). On denoting. *Mind, 14*(56), 479–493. https://doi.org/10.1093/wbro/lkj004

Saeed, J. I. (2003). *Semantics* (2nd edition). Malden, MA: Blackwell.

Scheffler, P. (2007). Ćwiczenia tłumaczeniowe w nowoczesnym nauczaniu języków obcych. *Języki Obce w Szkole,* (3), 58–62.

Scheffler, P. (2011). Rule difficulty: Teachers' intuitions and learners' performance. *Language Awareness, 20*(3), 221–237. https://doi.org/10.1080/09658416.2011.570349

Schmitt, N., Grandage, S., & Adolphs, S. (2004). Are corpus-derived recurrent clusters psycholinguistically valid? In N. Schmitt (Ed.), *Formulaic sequences: Acquisition, processing and use* (pp. 127–152). Amsterdam: John Benjamins.

Schwartz, B. D., & Sprouse, R. (1996). L2 cognitive states and the full transfer/full access model. *Second Language Research, 12*, 40–72.

Segalowitz, N. (2003). Automaticity and second languages. In C. Doughty & M. H. Long (Eds.), *The handbook of second language acquisition* (pp. 382–408). Malden: Blackwell.

Segalowitz, N. (2005). Automaticity in bilingualism and second language learning. In F. Kroll & A. M. B. de Groot (Eds.), *Handbook of bilingualism: Psycholinguistic approaches* (pp. 371–388). New York: Oxford University Press.

Sheen, Y. (2007a). The effect of corrective feedback, language aptitude and learner attitudes on the acquisition of English articles. In A. Mackey (Ed.), *Conversational interaction in second language acquisition* (pp. 301–322). Oxford: Oxford University Press.

Sheen, Y. (2007b). The effect of focused written corrective feedback and language aptitude on ESL learners' acquisition of articles. *Tesol Quarterly*, *41*(2), 255–283. https://doi.org/10.1002/j.1545-7249.2007.tb00059.x

Shin, Y. K., & Kim, Y. (2017). Using lexical bundles to teach articles to L2 English learners of different proficiencies. *System*, *69*, 79–91. https://doi.org/10.1016/j.system.2017.08.002

Shintani, N., & Ellis, R. (2013). The comparative effect of direct written corrective feedback and metalinguistic explanation on learners' explicit and implicit knowledge of the English indefinite article. *Journal of Second Language Writing*, *22*(3), 286–306. https://doi.org/10.1016/j.jslw.2013.03.011

Shintani, N., Ellis, R., & Suzuki, W. (2014). Effects of written feedback and revision on learners' accuracy in using two English grammatical structures. *Language Learning*, *64*(1), 103–131. https://doi.org/10.1111/lang.12029

Silva, L. H. R., & Roehr-Brackin, K. (2016). Perceived learning difficulty and actual performance: Explicit and implicit knowledge of L2 English grammar points among instructed adult learners. *Studies in Second Language Acquisition*, *38*(2), 317–340. https://doi.org/10.1017/S0272263115000340

Sinclair, J. (Ed.). (1990). *The Collins Cobuild English grammar*. London: Harper Collins.

Sinclair, J. (1991). *Corpus, concordance, collocation*. Oxford: Oxford University Press.

Singleton, D. (1999). *Exploring the second language mental lexicon*. Cambridge: Cambridge University Press.

Singleton, D. (2000). *Language and the lexicon*. London, New York: Arnold.

Singleton, D., Leśniewska, J., & Witalisz, E. (2007). Open choice versus the idiom principle in L2 lexical usage. In M. Pawlak (Ed.), *Exploring focus on form in language teaching* (pp. 207–222). Poznań, Kalisz: Adam Mickiewicz University.

Siyanova-Chanturia, A., Conklin, K., & van Heuven, W. J. B. (2011). Seeing a phrase "time and again" matters: The role of phrasal frequency in the processing of multiword sequences. *Journal of Experimental Psychology: Learning Memory and Cognition*, *37*(3), 776–784. https://doi.org/10.1037/a0022531

Siyanova-Chanturia, A., & Martinez, R. (2015). The idiom principle revisited. *Applied Linguistics*, *36*(5), 549–569. https://doi.org/10.1093/applin/amt054

Skehan, P. (1998). *A cognitive approach to language learning*. Oxford, New York: Oxford University Press.

Snape, N. (2008). Resetting the Nominal Mapping Parameter in L2 English: Definite article use and the count–mass distinction. *Bilingualism: Language and Cognition*, 11(1), 63–79. https://doi.org/10.1017/S1366728907003215

Sosa, A. V., & MacFarlane, J. (2002). Evidence for frequency-based constituents in the mental lexicon: Collocations involving the word *of. Brain and Language*, 83(2), 227–236. https://doi.org/10.1016/S0093-934X(02)00032-9

Spada, N., & Tomita, Y. (2010). Interactions between type of instruction and type of language feature: A meta-analysis. *Language Learning*, 60(2), 263–308.

Sperber, D., & Wilson, D. (1995). *Relevance: communication and cognition* (2nd edition). Oxford: Blackwell.

Stefanou, C., & Révész, A. (2015). Direct written corrective feedback, learner differences, and the acquisition of second language article use for generic and specific plural reference. *The Modern Language Journal*, 99(2), 263–282. https://doi.org/10.1111/modl.12212

Stubbs, M. (2009). The search for units of meaning: Sinclair on empirical semantics. *Applied Linguistics*, 30(1), 115–137.

Sun, G. (2016). The acquisition of English articles by second language learners: The sequence, differences, and difficulties. *SAGE Open*, 6(1). https://doi.org/ https://journals.sagepub.com/doi/pdf/10.1177/2158244016635716

Świątek, A. (2013). The acquisition of the English article system by Polish learners in different proficiency groups juxtaposed with a case study. In E. Piechurska-Kuciel & E. Szymańska-Czaplak (Eds.), *Language in cognition and affect* (pp. 151–170). Berlin, Heidelberg: Springer.

Świątek, A. (2014). *The order of the acquisition of the English article system by Polish learners in different proficiency groups*. Newcastle upon Tyne: Cambridge Scholars Publishing.

Szwedek, A. (1973). Some aspects of definiteness and indefiniteness of nouns in Polish. *Papers and Studies in Contrastive Linguistics*, 2, 203–212.

Szwedek, A. (1976). *Word order, sentence stress and reference in English and Polish*. Edmonton: Linguistic Research.

Tabossi, P., Fanari, R., & Wolf, K. (2009). Why are idioms recognized fast? *Memory and Cognition*, 37(4), 529–540. https://doi.org/10.3758/MC.37.4.529

Tarone, E., & Parrish, B. (1988). Task-related variation in interlanguage: The case of articles. *Language Learning*, 38(1), 21–44.

Thomas, M. (1989). The acquisition of English articles by first- and second-language learners. *Applied Psycholinguistics*, 10(3), 335–355. https://doi.org/10.1017/S0142716400008663

Tomasello, M. (2003). *Constructing a language: A usage-based theory of language acquisition.* Cambridge, London: Harvard University Press.

Towell, R., Hawkins, R., & Bazergui, N. (1996). The development of fluency in advanced learners of French. *Applied Linguistics, 17*(1), 84–119.

Tremblay, A., & Baayen, R. H. (2010). Holistic processing of regular four-word sequences: A behavioral and ERP study of the effects of structure, frequency, and probability on immediate free recall. In D. Wood (Ed.), *Perspectives on formulaic language: Acquisition and communication* (pp. 151–173). London: Continuum International.

Tremblay, A., Derwing, B., Libben, G., & Westbury, C. (2011). Processing advantages of lexical bundles: Evidence from self-paced reading and sentence recall tasks. *Language Learning, 61*(2), 569–613. https://doi.org/10.1111/j.1467-9922.2010.00622.x

Trenkic, D. (2007). Variability in second language article production: Beyond the representational deficit vs. processing constraints debate. *Second Language Research, 23*(3), 289–327. https://doi.org/10.1177/0267658307077643

Trenkic, D. (2008). The representation of English articles in second language grammars: Determiners or adjectives? *Bilingualism: Language and Cognition, 11*(1), 1–18. https://doi.org/10.1017/S1366728907003185

Tyler, A. (2012). *Cognitive linguistics and second language learning: Theoretical basics and experimental evidence.* New York, London: Routledge.

Vainikka, A., & Young-Scholten, M. (1996). Gradual development of L2 phrase structure. *Second Language Research, 12,* 7–39.

Van Lancker, D., Canter, G., & Terbeek, D. (1981). Disambiguation of ditropic sentences. *Journal of Speech, Language, and Hearing Research, 24*(3), 330–335. https://doi.org/10.1044/jshr.2403.330

Van Lancker, D., & Kempler, D. (1987). Comprehension of familiar phrases by left- but not by right-hemisphere damaged patients. *Brain and Language, 32,* 265–277.

Van Lancker-Sidtis, D. (2012). Formulaic language and language disorders. *Annual Review of Applied Linguistics, 32,* 62–80. https://doi.org/10.1017/S0267190512000104

Van Lancker-Sidtis, D., & Postman, W. A. (2006). Formulaic expressions in spontaneous speech of left- and right-hemisphere damaged subjects. *Aphasiology, 20,* 411–426.

Van Langendonck, W. (1994). Determiners as heads? *Cognitive Linguistics, 5*(3), 243–260.

Verneau, M., van der Kamp, J., Savelsbergh, G. J. P., & de Looze, M. P. (2014). Age and time effects on implicit and explicit learning. *Experimental Aging Research*, *40*(4), 477–511.

von Heusinger, K. (n.d.). Definiteness. In *Oxford Bibliographies*. Oxford University Press. https://doi.org/DOI: 10.1093/OBO/9780199772810-0063

Warden, D. A. (1976). The influence of context on children's use of identifying expressions and references. *British Journal of Psychology*, *67*(1), 101–112.

Weinert, R. (1995). The role of formulaic language in second language acquisition: A review. *Applied Linguistics*, *16*(2), 180–205. https://doi.org/10.1093/applin/16.2.180

White, B. (2009). Accounting for L2-English learners' article choices. *MSU Working Papers in SLS*, *1*(1), 14–37.

White, B. (2012). A conceptual approach to the instruction of phrasal verbs. *The Modern Language Journal*, *96*(3), 419–438. https://doi.org/10.1111/j.1540-4781.2012.01365.x

White, L. (1989). *Universal grammar and second language acquisition*. Amsterdam: John Benjamins.

Wierzbicka, A. (1988). *The semantics of grammar*. Amsterdam, Philadelphia: John Benjamins.

Wolter, B., & Gyllstad, H. (2013). Frequency of input and L2 collocational processing. *Studies in Second Language Acquisition*, *35*(3), 451–482. https://doi.org/10.1017/S0272263113000107

Wolter, B., & Yamashita, Y. (2018). Word frequency, collocational frequency, L1 congruency, and proficiency in L2 collocational processing: What accounts for L2 performance? *Studies in Second Language Acquisition*, *40*(2), 395–416. https://doi.org/10.1017/S0272263117000237

Wong-Fillmore, L. (1976). *The second time around: Cognitive and social strategies in second language acquisition* (doctoral dissertation). Stanford University.

Wray, A. (2002a). *Formulaic language and the lexicon*. Cambridge: Cambridge University Press.

Wray, A. (2002b). Formulaic language in computer-supported communication: Theory meets reality. *Language Awareness*, *11*(2), 114–131. https://doi.org/10.1080/09658410208667050

Wray, A. (2012). What do we (think we) know about formulaic language? An evaluation of the current state of play. *Annual Review of Applied Linguistics*, *32*, 231–254. https://doi.org/10.1017/S026719051200013X

Yalçın, Ş., & Spada, N. (2016). Language aptitude and grammatical difficulty. *Studies in Second Language Acquisition, 38*(2), 239–263. https://doi.org/10.1017/S0272263115000509

Yamada, J., & Matsuura, N. (1982). The use of the English article among Japanese students. *RELC Journal, 13*(1), 50–63. https://doi.org/10.1177/003368828201300104

Yamashita, J., & Jiang, N. (2010). L1 influence on the acquisition of L2 collocations : Japanese ESL users and EFL learners acquiring English collocations. *TESOL Quarterly, 44*(4), 647–668.

Yoo, I. W. (2009). The English definite article: What ESL/EFL grammars say and what corpus findings show. *Journal of English for Academic Purposes, 8*(4), 267–278. https://doi.org/10.1016/j.jeap.2009.07.004

Yoon, K. K. (1993). Challenging prototype descriptions: Perception of noun countability and indefinite vs. zero article use. *IRAL: International Review of Applied Linguistics in Language Teaching, 31*(4), 269–289.

Yorio, C. (1989). Idiomaticity as an indicator of second language proficiency. In K. Hyltenstam & L. K. Obler (Eds.), *Bilingualism across the lifespan: Aspects of acquisition, maturity and loss* (pp. 55–72). New York: Oxford University Press. https://doi.org/https://doi.org/10.1017/CBO9780511611780.005

Young, R. (1996). Form-function relations in articles in English interlanguage. In R. Bayley & D. R. Preston (Eds.), *Second language acquisition and linguistic variation* (pp. 135–175). Amsterdam: John Benjamins. https://doi.org/10.1075/sibil.10.07you

Yule, G. (1998). *Explaining English grammar.* Oxford: Oxford University Press.

Zabor, L., & Rychlewska, A. (2015). The effectiveness of written corrective feedback in the acquisition of the English article system by Polish learners in view of the counterbalance hypothesis. In L. Piasecka, M. Adams-Tukiendorf, & P. Wilk (Eds.), *New media and perennial problems in foreign language learning and teaching* (pp. 131–150). Berlin: Springer.

Zdorenko, T., & Paradis, J. (2008). The acquisition of articles in child second language English: Fluctuation, transfer or both? *Second Language Research, 24*(2), 227–250. https://doi.org/10.1177/0267658307086302

Appendix 1

The text below does not have articles. Write the articles in the correct places, as in the example.

Example: He is ⌄most wonderful person I've ever met.

the

1. Motorised boats harm ecology of waterways, unless their use is kept at low level.
2. Glucose, or blood sugar, is produced in our bodies when we eat carbohydrates.
3. We meet regularly, five times semester, at departmental meeting.
4. Time matters. Please try to send it in as soon as possible – sooner better.
5. I want to choose foreign language that few people want to study. Maybe I'll learn Kurdish.
6. Plants in pots and containers require more water than you actually might think, smaller pot more critical problem. By midsummer, herbs and vegetables in containers may need water twice day.
7. You should give him spoonful of this syrup every three hours.

8. I'll remember you until day I die.
9. I see that you haven't eaten any of food I brought you two days ago. Can I make you cup of tea?
10. Old leftist political parties are re-emerging to demand that government again expand its role in economy to help poor, even at price of discouraging foreign investors.
11. I was lucky ball didn't hit me in face.
12. New version of insurance policy makes number of alternatives open to insured.
13. Do you speak English?
14. I was recently asked about my hopes for future by friend of mine. What I know is that I'd like to have kids. And I'd like to live in luxury apartment one day.
15. Immediately after graduation I need to get job. It doesn't necessarily have to be in my field, and I'm prepared to move anywhere where I can find work. Acquaintance of mine was recently offered position in Berlin and he moved there without moment's hesitation.
16. What remarkable player he is. His performance today really impressed me. What shame he didn't get picked for team.
17. Every member of Royal Family enjoys star status; they are used to being centre of attention and there is strong unstated rivalry between them.
18. He was cut in hand in same fight, according to testimony.

Appendix 2

STUDY 1: TEST ITEMS AND THEIR FREQUENCY IN BNC AND COCA

Pair	Version A/B	Article	Target phrase	Frequency	BNC 100,000,000		COCA 450,000,000	
					raw	per million	raw	per million
1.	Version A:	a	a friend of mine	High	230	2.30	1,327	2.95
	Version B:		an acquaintance of mine	Low	1	0.01	33	0.07
2.	Version A:	a	what a shame	High	120	1.20	173	0.38
	Version B:		what a remarkable player	Low	0	0.00	0	0.00
3.	Version A:	a	twice a day	High	142	1.42	754	1.68
	Version B:		five times a semester	Low	0	0.00	0	0.00
4.	Version A:	the	the sooner the better*	High	28	0.28	135	0.30
	Version B:		the smaller the pot, the more critical the problem	Low	1	0.01	0	0.00
5.	Version A:	a	a cup of tea	High	619	6.19	876	1.95
	Version B:		a spoonful of syrup	Low	0	0.00	1	0.00
6.	Version A:	the	the day I die	High	11	0.11	81	0.18
	Version B:		the food I brought	Low	0	0.00	1	0.00
7.	Version A:	the	help the poor	High	21	0.21	241	0.54
	Version B:		open to the insured	Low	2	0.02	0	0.00
8.	Version A:	the	hit (someone) in the face	High	26	0.26	115	0.26
	Version B:		cut in the hand	Low	0	0.00	2	0.00

Pair	Version A/B	Article	Target phrase	Frequency	BNC 100,000,000 raw	per million	COCA 450,000,000 raw	per million
9.	Version A:	zero	speak English	High	174	1.74	1,328	2.95
	Version B:		learn Kurdish	Low	0	0.00	0	0.00
10.	Version A:	a	get a job	High	299	2.99	1,749	3.89
	Version B:		live in a luxury apartment	Low	0	0.00	0	0.00
11.	Version A:	zero	have kids	High	42	0.42	1,158	2.57
	Version B:		eat carbohydrates	Low	0	0.00	11	0.02
12.	Version A:	the	the centre of attention**	High	85	0.85	392	0.87
	Version B:		the ecology of waterways	Low	1	0.01	0	0.00

⋆ The frequency count includes both punctuation versions: *the sooner the better* and *the sooner, the better.*
⋆⋆ The frequency count includes both the spelling *center* and *centre.*

Appendix 3

The sentences and texts below do not have articles. Write the articles in the correct places, as in the example.

Example: He is ∨most wonderful person I've ever met.
<small>the</small>

1. I often wake up in middle of night.
2. Smoking cigarettes results in 30-fold increase in chance of contracting lung cancer.
3. I think I'll have nightmares about it for rest of my life.
4. People should be judged on merit of their character.
5. There are many interesting places in distant north where you can experience true arctic winter.
6. He made some final corrections and few slight changes in phrasing of his report, and then sent it to his boss.
7. This magazine has strong position in nexus of global multi-national media.
8. He was waiting for me at top of stairs.

9. Building which you can see on far edge of square is university library.
10. They were discussing political situation in Middle East.
11. Small-group activities, though requiring more work on part of instructor, can be effective strategy for promoting classroom engagement.
12. If you look at underside of your laptop, you should find sticker certifying authenticity of software installed on device.
13. Our approach to university admissions relies on factor of competition.
14. Please tell us where you were at time of explosion.
15. He was slowing down as race went on, but then he found new energy for last lap.
16. Evaluating teachers largely on basis of student test scores is not good idea.

TEXT 1:

It was invention of lifts that made skiing popular. Before then, people would have to hike up mountains to ski down them. Although skiing has existed in one form or another for thousands of years, motorized lifts came into use only at beginning of 20th century. First known working lift, in form of water-powered tow rope for skiers and toboggans, operated during winter of 1908 in German town of Schonaich, in Black Forest. It took bit longer for lifts to appear in United States, but by mid-1930s, tows made from old auto parts were fairly common in New England. At same time, cable cars (which had been used in mining for several hundred years) became commonly used to transport skiers.

Here are some of things that you should remember when preparing for your first skiing holiday. When learning to ski, it is important to choose slopes which are at right level of difficulty. When buying or renting skis, select skis with radius that's appropriate for width of slopes you typically ski on.

TEXT 2:

Around 20,000 people live in Kuril Islands, chain of islands connecting northernmost part of Japan to tip of Russia's Kamchatka Peninsula. Islands look like dotted line on one side of which lies vast Pacific Ocean; on other side is Sea of Okhotsk. Islands have been claimed by both Russia and Japan. Two countries established diplomatic relations for first time in 1855. Since then, they have traded possession of islands. Treaty of Saint Petersburg, signed in 1875 at closure of very long negotiations, gave islands to Japan in exchange for island of Sakhalin. Soviet Union conquered islands at end of World War II. At period of Cold War, Japan made claim that four southernmost islands should be returned to Japan. For Russian leaders disputed islands play important role in context of defence planning, as without them it is impossible to control access to Sea of Okhotsk. Some attempts at negotiations were made by two countries at dawning of new millennium.

TECHNICAL EDITOR
Karolina Wąsowska

PROOFREADER
Małgorzata Szul

TYPESETTER
Marta Jaszczuk

Jagiellonian University Press
Editorial Offices: ul. Michałowskiego 9/2, 31-126 Kraków
Phone: +48 12 663 23 80, Fax: +48 12 663 23 83

GPSR Authorized Representative: Easy Access System Europe, Mustamäe tee
50, 10621 Tallinn, Estonia, gpsr.requests@easproject.com

www.ingramcontent.com/pod-product-compliance
Lightning Source LLC
Chambersburg PA
CBHW061733120626
46550CB00005B/1790